P9-EMG-934

DATE DUE

the AMAZING story of Creation

from science and the Bible

DUANE T. GISH

Illustrated by
Earl and Bonnie Snellenberger

Institute for Creation Research
P.O. Box 2667
El Cajon, CA   92021

The Amazing Story of CREATION from science and the Bible

Institute for Creation Research
P.O. Box 2667
El Cajon, CA 92021

Library of Congress Catalog Card Number 90-082827   **ISBN** 0-89051-120-9

Printed in the United States of America

the AMAZING story of
CREATION
from science and the Bible

TABLE OF CONTENTS

This book is dedicated to my three wonderful grandsons, Alex and Ben Slaughter, and Carson Gish.

ABOUT THE AUTHOR

Dr. Duane Gish is a man who, in addition to his accomplishments as a speaker and writer, is known by many as the foremost creationist debater in the world today. He has logged literally hundreds of thousands of miles in order to bring the truth of creation to adults and children alike. Dr. Gish's travels have taken him to virtually every state in the continental U.S. and into 25 foreign countries, including the Soviet Union.

Dr. Duane T. Gish

His book, *Dinosaurs: Those Terrible Lizards*, was published when there was very little creationist literature available for children. *Evolution: The Challenge of the Fossil Record* is the book God has used in the lives of many to lay aside, once and for all, the fallacious ape-man theory.

Dr. Gish received his Ph.D. in biochemistry in 1953 from the University of California, Berkeley. He has held key positions at Berkeley, Cornell University Medical College, and The Upjohn Company, where he collaborated with former Nobel Prize winners in various projects. His interest in the creation/evolution issue grew until, in 1971, he left The Upjohn Company to join the faculty at the newly established (1970) Christian Heritage College and its research division. In 1972, the latter changed its name to the Institute for Creation Research, and Dr. Gish has served as Associate Director and Vice President since that time.

Dr. Gish is listed in AMERICAN MEN OF SCIENCE and WHO'S WHO IN THE WEST. He is a member of the American Chemical Society, the American Association for the Advancement of Science, and is a Fellow of the American Institute of Chemists.

"Remember now thy Creator in the days of thy youth."
This wise advice was given long ago by King Solomon, of
whom it was said that "all the earth sought to Solomon, to
hear his wisdom, which God had put in his heart" (I Kings
10:24). Even more significant is the fact that God included it
in the Bible (Ecclesiastes 12:1), so that it actually is a command
of God.

If possible, it is more important today than even in
Solomon's time for young people to learn about their Creator
while they are still young. Most of our public schools, as well
as most media today, promote the idea that all things have
happened by a slow, chance process of *evolution*.

But this is not true at all. God specially *created* the world
and all the different kinds of plants and animals. Most
importantly of all, He created the first man and woman (Adam
and Eve) directly, not by a long process of evolution from an
ape-like ancestor, but simply by His own power. He has even
created an eternal soul for each one of us, because He loves us
and has a special purpose for each of us in this world.

This truth of special creation is plainly taught in God's
Word, the Bible. It is also clearly taught in the creation itself,
and in all the scientific facts which have been discovered about
the creation by scientists. The author of this book, Dr. Duane
Gish, is himself a renowned scientist who has been studying
these evidences for many years, and has spoken to many
audiences about them—not only to young people, but to large
groups of scientists and other adults as well. Now he wants
to share some of his lecture materials with young people
everywhere through this fascinating, beautifully illustrated
book.

Dr. Gish is not only a distinguished scientist, but also a
gracious Christian gentleman. He loves children and young
people and earnestly wants to help them come to know and
follow their Creator and Savior. The talented artists who have
prepared many beautiful illustrations for the book, Earl and
Bonnie Snellenberger, have the same desire. So do all of us
here at the Institute for Creation Research and at Master Books.

The Amazing Story of Creation not only explains many of the
wonderful evidences for creation, but also encourages our
hearts and minds to worship our Creator and believe His Word.
Then—some day, when He comes again—we can all join in the
heavenly song: "Thou art worthy, O Lord, to receive glory and
honor and power: For Thou hast created all things, and for
Thy pleasure they are and were created" (Revelation 4:11).

Henry M. Morris
San Diego, California
June, 1990

5

CREATION AND EVOLUTION TWO DIFFERENT VIEWS OF ORIGINS

How did everything get started? Where did we come from? Whatever happened to the dinosaurs? What about cavemen? Have you ever wondered about such things? Of course you have. We all have.

Where can we find the answers to these and other questions? Should we ask scientists or should we believe the Bible? Can we do both?

As a Christian, I believe that *God created*, just as He tells us in the *Bible*. In the very first verse of the Bible, we find out that "In the beginning God created the heavens and the earth." God wants us to know right from the start that He has created us. Before He told us anything else, He made it plain that we didn't come about by accident. The fact that we were created by God is one of the most important things that we learn from the Bible.

The Bible is not the only place that we can learn about creation, however. The facts of *science* also tell us much about creation. By carefully studying the facts of science, I have become convinced that the universe could not have created itself, and that living things, including people, could not have happened just by chance—*they had to be created by God*!

"The heavens declare the glory of God; and the firmament shows His handiwork." *Psalm* 19:1

Most people, including thousands of scientists, believe that God created everything, but there are others, even many scientists, who don't believe that God created our wonderful universe. These people believe that the stars and planets created themselves by natural processes, and that all plants and animals happened by accident. They don't believe that God created men and women or that the world was created to be a home for them. They say, "Things just happen to be the way they are; there is no real purpose in our being here; we got here by chance." This idea is called the *theory of evolution*, and the people who believe in it are called *evolutionists*. Those of us who believe that God created everything believe in *creation*. We are called *creationists*.

What the Bible tells us about God and how He created us is very different from what the theory of evolution says. Therefore, no one can really believe what the Bible tells us about creation and also believe in evolution. It may be a surprise to a lot of people, but *neither can one really believe in the facts of science and believe in evolution!* Evolutionists claim belief in evolution because science supports evolution. To say this is to be either ignorant of the truth (the real facts of science), or to deny creation no matter what the facts say, because in order to believe in creation, one has to believe in God. There are people who don't want to believe in God and what the Bible says because belief requires accountability. No matter what evolutionists want to believe, however, the facts of science do not support evolution. On the other hand, there is a mountain of scientific evidence that supports creation.

Why, then, do most of the books used in public schools teach only evolution? Why is it that most books and such magazines as the *National Geographic* rarely mention the possibility of creation? Why is it that television programs usually talk about evolution and only rarely about the scientific evidence for creation? The reason is that most people who write books for schools and articles for magazines, and who make up TV programs don't believe in creation, and either do not want people to hear the scientific evidence for creation, or are themselves ignorant about the true facts of science.

Yet, even though there are more creationists than evolutionists in the United States, evolutionism pervades everything that is taught in our schools and what we see in the media. Many evolutionists are afraid to let the evidence speak for itself or to present the many facts of science that support creation. Evolutionists hold to their theory because the alternative is belief in a Creator.

Even though we have a democracy in the United States (which means "majority rule"), it doesn't always work out that way. Sometimes our democracy doesn't extend into the classroom. In a poll taken in 1981, people in the United States were asked if they wanted creation taught in the schools. About 76 percent said they wanted **both** creation and evolution taught in the schools. About ten percent wanted only creation to be taught. That means that 86 percent of the people in the United States want creation taught in our public schools! Only eight percent said they wanted only evolution taught (the other six percent couldn't make up their minds). Even though 86 percent of the American people want the scientific evidence for creation taught in schools, the science textbooks used in our schools teach only evolution. If school children were allowed to study the evidence and choose for themselves whether it best fits the theory of evolution or that of creation, we would have better science, better thinkers, and, in the end, better schools.

Science is very interesting, and learning how the facts about our world support creation is truly an *amazing* story. Both the Bible and science tell us about how the universe came into existence; how stars, galaxies, and planets were formed; how plants and animals—all these living things came into existence, and these facts are marvelous support for creation! In this book, we will learn about dinosaurs, and how dinosaur fossils give evidence against evolution and in support of creation.

What about the origin of man? Did we really come from apes, like evolutionists tell us? Can we believe that and also believe what the Bible says? Do the facts of science give evidence that we evolved from apes, or do the facts of science show that God created man as man, right from the start? The Bible and science both have a lot to say about these things. Yes, science tells us that man—*Homo sapiens*—has always been man.

9

Chapter 1

WHO MADE THE STARS?

In the Beginning, Light!

And God said, Let there be light: and there was light. And God saw the light, that it was good: And God divided the light from the darkness. And God called the light Day, and the darkness He called Night. And the evening and the morning were the first day.

Genesis 1:3-5

And God made two great lights; the greater light to rule the day, and the lesser light to rule the night: He made the stars also.

Genesis 1:16

Solar flare

Milky Way

Who made the stars? God made the stars. There is only one way we know stars exist, besides, of course, the fact that the Bible says God created them. We can't touch stars, or smell them, or hear them. But we can *see* them! And we see them because they give off light.

11

There is another reason that light is very important. Light is energy. Almost all the energy we use here on the earth comes

"Light is energy."

from the light energy we get from the sun. Plants can grow because they get light energy from the sun. You and I get energy either from the plants we eat or from the animals we eat, such as chickens and cattle, which get their energy from eating plants. Even the coal and oil we burn for energy comes from plants and animals which get their energy from the sun. The universe and everything in it would be dead without energy, and almost all the energy we have on the earth comes from the sun.

If you read verses 14-19 of the first chapter of Genesis, you will discover that God didn't create the sun, the moon and the stars until the fourth day of creation. How, then, could there have been light on the first day of creation, when the sun and the stars did not yet exist? It is true that all light in the universe comes from the stars, including our own star, the sun; but it wasn't so in the beginning. Remember, light is energy. On the first day, God created the most important thing of all—light energy. Nothing can operate without energy, and this energy was light. The universe was full of light, even though our sun and the stars didn't exist yet.

There is another reason energy is important. Matter is a form of energy. Energy can be changed into matter, and matter can be changed into energy. In the explosion of a hydrogen bomb, most of the hydrogen changes into helium, but a small amount changes into energy. When that little bit of hydrogen changes into energy, enough is produced to blow up a mountain or to destroy an entire city the size of New York City.

It is also possible to change energy into matter, although it is very difficult, and takes a very powerful machine, called a cyclotron.

God created light, or energy, on the first day of creation *ex nihilo* ("out of nothing"). The Bible tells us that it wasn't until the fourth day of Creation Week that God made the moon, the sun, and all the stars. God made the sun to give us light so we could see and have energy for life. God made the moon as the "lesser light to rule the night" (Genesis 1:16). The sun's diameter is about four hundred times that of the moon, and its distance from the earth is also about four hundred times that of the moon. This means that the moon is just exactly large enough to cover the sun's disc at the time of a total eclipse. We do not know why God chose this particular size and placement of these two spheres, but we can be sure this is no coincidence! The Bible also tells us that God made the stars to be for signs and for seasons.

It is believed that some of the stars are so far away that it would take millions or billions of years for the light to reach the earth from the stars, even though light travels at a speed of 186,000 miles per second! How, then, could the stars serve as signs and seasons on the earth if these stars were created on the fourth day of creation and man was created on the sixth day? Would man have had to wait many millions of years before he could see the stars? When God created the stars, He also could easily have created the stream of light between the stars and the earth. Thus, Adam and Eve could "see" each star and know exactly where it was in the sky on the very first night when they looked up into the sky. You might say that the light beam coming to the earth from each star serves as a "pointer" to tell us where each star is.

Big Bang theory

Evolutionists don't believe that God created the universe with all the stars and planets, but, of course, they weren't there when the universe came into existence. They don't believe what God tells us about how He created everything, so evolutionists can only try to imagine how the universe came to be.

One idea that evolutionists have is called the "Big Bang" theory. According to this theory, billions of years ago there weren't any stars, or planets, or people, or anything else. All of the energy and matter in the universe was crammed together

13

in a big ball, or "cosmic egg." Where did the cosmic egg come from? How did it get there? No one knows.

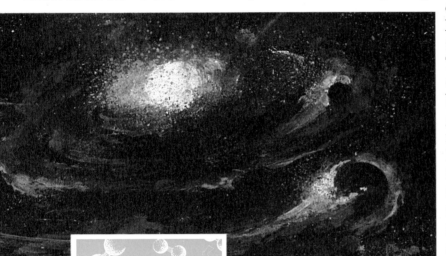

Theoretical star creation

For some reason, evolutionists believe, the cosmic egg exploded with a "big bang." How long was it there before it exploded? Why did it explode? No one knows. Evolutionists *imagine* that all of this happened. This "big bang" supposedly created hydrogen gas. If a balloon is filled with hydrogen gas and released, it will rapidly rise, because hydrogen is much lighter than air. In fact, hydrogen is the lightest substance known to man. Evolutionists believe that the hydrogen gas created by the big bang expanded, or spread out, into all the universe—that there weren't any stars, or planets, or galaxies at that time—that there was nothing in the entire universe except hydrogen gas. In fact, evolutionists could say that hydrogen gas *was* the universe!

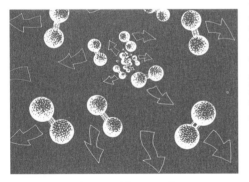

Gravitational attraction

Where did the stars and planets come from? How did they form? Evolutionists imagine that somehow stars created themselves from hydrogen gas. They believe that the hydrogen molecules in a certain area of space began to pull in on themselves by gravity. This area is thought to have been very large, as much as six trillion miles across! All of the molecules within this space started moving toward each other. In other words, as the cloud of gas got smaller and smaller and the molecules of gas got closer and closer, the cloud of gas got hotter and hotter, and finally, evolutionists tell us, the cloud of gas got so hot, it became a star.

Expansion of heated gases

Actually, there is a very simple reason why this could never happen and why stars cannot create themselves. A cloud of gas is spread out, and is very cold. When a cloud of gas contracts, however, the molecules get closer together. When this happens, the gas gets hotter. Two things happen: The gas molecules pull in on one another, by gravity, and this tends to make the cloud of gas contract, or get smaller. At the same time, however, because the cloud of gas is getting hotter, gas pressure is pushing out, and tends to make the cloud of gas expand, or get bigger. Gravity pulls in, but gas pressure pushes out.

14

If the cloud of gas is going to collapse, or sink in on itself to make a star, the gravity pulling in has to be stronger than the gas pressure pushing out. Scientists have ways of calculating these two forces. It turns out that the gas pressure pushing out is almost 100 times stronger than the gravity pulling in! Instead of the cloud of gas getting smaller and smaller until it forms a star, it would get bigger and bigger, and a star could never create itself.

One evolutionist wrote an article about the problem of the formation of stars. He admitted that the gas pressure pushing

Observatory

out would be stronger than gravity pulling in, and that a star could not create itself that way. However, he said, maybe a nearby star would explode (a supernova), and the explosion would give enough push on the cloud of hydrogen gas to overcome the gas pressure, and this would make the star. This theory has one *BIG* problem: To have a supernova, you have to have a star. According to this theory, one has to have stars to make stars! And stars cannot create themselves. That means they had to *be* created.

Observatory control room

Before telescopes were invented, people looked up into the sky and saw what they believed to be stars. When astronomers began to use telescopes, they discovered that many of the "stars" were not individual stars, but were great *groups* of stars. These groups of stars are called *galaxies*. Astronomers believe that there may be as many as 100 billion stars in each galaxy! Our own star, the sun, is part of the Milky Way galaxy.

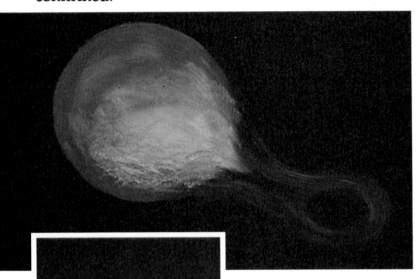

Radio telescopes allow us to see farther into space than conventional telescopes.

Astronomers also believe that the universe may contain as many as 100 billion galaxies! This shouldn't come as any big surprise. God has no limit! If He wanted to, He could create a universe with an infinite number of galaxies.

In many ways, the universe is still very mysterious to astronomers. For example, in addition to ordinary stars and galaxies, there are strange objects, such as quasars. Astronomers still don't know what quasars are, except that they believe they are very far away, and that they produce a lot of energy. Astronomers have also identified what they call "black holes." This is only speculation, because no one has ever seen a black hole. Black holes are supposed to be places where matter has become so tightly packed that gravity is almost infinite. Gravity is so great, it is thought, that nothing can get out of these black holes—not even light can escape. Since not even light can escape from a "black hole," no one can see one, and, therefore, it cannot be confirmed scientifically whether they do exist. However, some astronomers still believe that such things exist, but many do not. If they do, perhaps that is what Christ meant when He talked of a place of outer darkness (Matthew 8:12).

There are many, many things that we will never know about the universe until we go to heaven and have the opportunity to learn about it from its Creator. The universe is so immense and mysterious, we can really know very little about it until God tells us. It is possible to send a spacecraft to other planets in the Solar System. We have already put astronauts on the moon, and we have put spacecraft on Mars, but it is unlikely that we will ever be able to visit places outside of the Solar System. Why? Because all other stars, which might have planets, are too far away. The nearest star to our Solar System is Alpha Centauri (actually a combination of at least two stars). Alpha Centauri is 30 trillion miles from us! Assuming that a spacecraft traveled at 30 thousand miles per hour, it would take more than a million years to reach the nearest star. Even if a spacecraft could travel a thousand times faster, or 30 million miles per hour, it would still take over one thousand years to get to Alpha Centauri. "For as the heavens are higher than the earth, so are My ways higher than your ways, and My thoughts than your thoughts" (Isaiah 55:9). Because we know that God's wisdom is infinitely greater than ours, we can know that the "heavens" (the stars and space) stretch out infinitely beyond our earth. Astronomers have calculated there are 10^{25} stars (that is ten million billion billion) and the Bible indicates God has named them all individually. (Psalm 147:4; Isaiah 40:26).

The universe is like a giant machine. It is not only very large and complex, it is very orderly. One astronomer said that whoever was responsible for the universe must have been a marvelous mathematician.

According to evolutionists, our incredibly complex, wonderfully orderly, mathematically precise universe was created by an explosion! Has anyone ever seen an explosion create order? Of course not! Explosions don't create order, they just leave a mess. Sir Fred Hoyle, one of the world's most famous astronomers, no longer believes in the Big Bang theory. He says that no stars, no planets, no galaxies—nothing like that—could ever come out of such a "big bang." Sir Fred Hoyle used to be an atheist and an evolutionist, but now he believes that life had to be created! If such a world-famous astronomer believes it is impossible that a big bang theory could have created the universe, there are a lot of good scientific reasons to believe that the universe did not create itself. God created the universe, exactly as we are told in the Bible.

Horse Head Nebula

Sir Fred Hoyle

17

Chapter **2**

CREATION OF THE EARTH

How Did the Planets Form?

We could say that the Solar System works just like a clock. Could you ever make a clock by accident? Do explosions in a jewelry shop create watches? Even if you put all the parts of a watch in a bag and shook the bag for billions and billions of years, would you ever get a watch? No! You would just wear out the parts. Starting with a cloud of dust and gas, then, could this wonderful, marvelously complex Solar System simply put itself together?

Evolutionists believe that about five billion years ago the Solar System was just a cloud of dust and gas, which they call the *solar nebula*. Where did the *solar nebula* come from? No one knows. What caused its rotation? No one knows that, either.

Evolutionists believe the cloud of gas and dust was spread out—maybe several trillion miles across—and it was very, very cold. Then, all those molecules of gas and dust began to pull in on themselves by gravity, and finally the sun became a star.

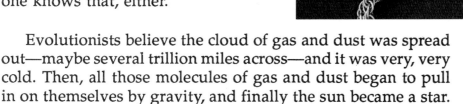

If gravity was great enough to pull in the sun, how could anything be left behind to make the planets? The sun weighs 1,000 times as much as all the planets combined—thus 99.9 percent of all the matter of the Solar System is in the sun. Some think that maybe dust and gas were left outside the cloud that formed the sun. This hypothetical cloud of dust and gas was orbiting the sun, and somehow, the dust particles and the gas got close enough to stick together and make planets. However, when one takes these ideas and compares them with the cold, hard facts of science, it can be proven that none of these imagined models could possibly work. Sir Herman Bondi, a noted British astronomer, admitted in an article published in the British Science Journal *New Scientist*, August 21, p.611 (1980) that all such theories have been proven wrong by scientific facts. Sir Harold Jeffreys, another well-known British astronomer, in a book published in 1970, said that since all of our theories about how the Solar System formed have been shown to be wrong, we can say it doesn't exist! Well, the Solar System *does* exist, and since science proves that it couldn't have created itself naturally, by some evolutionary process, there is only one possibility left! It had to be produced **supernaturally.** God made the Solar System, including the sun, the moon, and the earth, just as the Bible tells us.

Great Orion Nebula

Earth at the Beginning

And the earth was without form, and void; and darkness was upon the face of the deep. And the Spirit of God moved upon the face of the waters.

Earth rise from lunar surface.

And God said, Let the waters under the heaven be gathered together unto one place, and let the dry land appear: And it was so.

And God called the dry land Earth; and the gathering together of the waters called He Seas; and God saw that it was good.

Genesis 1:2,9,10

In Genesis 1:2 we are told that in the beginning the earth was without form, and void. The earth was void, or empty. God had not yet created any living things to live on the earth.

What is the Bible telling us, when it says that the earth was without form? Let us suppose that there is a vacant lot where someone is going to build a house. Suddenly, one day, you notice that the builder has placed bricks, sand, sacks of cement, lumber, and other building materials on the lot. At that time, we would say that the house is without form—it hasn't been built yet. And we could certainly say it is void, or empty. Obviously, no one can live in it yet. The house would be without form, and void, but that doesn't mean that it is in disorder or chaos! The bricks are perfect bricks; the lumber is perfect lumber; the cement is perfect; the pipes and other plumbing materials—the electrical wires and other building materials are all perfect, and everything has been placed in neat order on the building site.

That is the way it was in the beginning. Everything was there that God needed to make the earth, but He had not yet formed the earth and put living things on it.

The Bible tells us (Genesis 1:6-8) that God had separated the waters above the firmament from the waters below the firmament. You must understand that when the Old Testament was translated from Hebrew into English in about 1600 A.D. (the King James translation of the Bible), the word "firmament" meant "space." The Bible is telling us that God divided the waters so that some water was above the firmament, or space, and some water was on the earth (below the firmament, or space).

"And God said, Let the waters under the heaven be gathered together unto one place, and let the dry land appear: and it was so." *Genesis 1:9*

Water exists in three forms—liquid (ordinary water), solid (ice), and as a gas (water vapor). If you spill water on the floor, it soon disappears. It has evaporated—passed into the air and become invisible water vapor. The water in the sky is invisible water vapor, at least until it condenses to form rain.

Today, there is enough water on the earth so that if it were perfectly smooth, the entire earth would be covered with water almost two miles deep. Apparently, that is the way the earth was when God started to form the earth; but then God made continents and oceans. How did He do this? We weren't there, so we cannot know exactly what He did, but we can speculate.

Suppose you had a great ball of clay covered with water. Now, if in some places you push down the clay to make low places, or depressions, this would push the clay up, in other places. The low places, which would fill with water, would be the oceans, and the high places would be the continents. But whatever the method, God made the dry land, or continents, and the oceans, or seas. The earth was now ready for living things.

Our Amazing Planet

When we consider how beautiful our earth is today—how perfect it is for the existence of life—how everything still works for the benefit of human beings, and then remember that the earth is not nearly as wonderful as it was when God

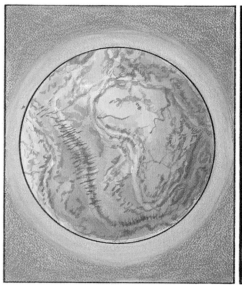

Earth's perfect distance from the Sun.

first created it, because of human sin, it is no wonder that God could look at the earth He had created and say, "It was very good."

There are many, many things that have to be just right on the earth, or life could not exist. If the earth were just a little bit closer to the sun, it would be too hot for life to exist. If the earth were a little bit farther away from the sun, it would be too cold; all the water on earth would be frozen solid, and there would be no life.

Water is absolutely essential for life, and on the earth we have 350 million cubic miles of water! But there is not a single drop of liquid water anywhere else in the Solar System! There is no liquid water on Mars, Venus, Mercury, or anywhere else—only on Earth.

The Protective Atmosphere

Oxygen is another significant element lacking elsewhere in our Solar System. Our atmosphere contains 21 percent of this life-giving oxygen, but there is no free oxygen on the moon, or on any other planet. We could not survive without it, but there is another very important reason for oxygen to exist on the earth. The ultraviolet light that is given off by the sun is deadly. Ultraviolet light has a lot of energy—so much energy that it kills living things. If bacteria are exposed to ultraviolet light they are killed in seconds! You and I and all other living things would die very quickly if we were exposed to the whole range of light coming from the sun, including the ultraviolet light. So God made sure that this wouldn't happen.

Ozone is produced from oxygen. The molecules of oxygen in our atmosphere have *two* atoms of oxygen, but in ozone, the molecules of oxygen have *three* atoms of oxygen. The ultraviolet light from the sun changes some of the ordinary molecules of oxygen, with *two* atoms of oxygen, into ozone with *three* atoms of oxygen. Now, ozone has a very special

Beauty and protection of the atmosphere.

property. Ozone absorbs ultraviolet light, so much of the ultraviolet light can't get through it. But there is a problem with ozone—it is poisonous! And just where is this ozone? Right where it *must* be to protect the earth from ultraviolet light. Ozone is found in a layer surrounding the earth about ten miles above the surface, where it can absorb and filter out the ultraviolet light from the sun, without messing up things down here on the earth.

The kind of light that plants need for energy and growth is visible light—the kind of light that can pass right through ozone. So ozone is perfect! It keeps out deadly, destructive ultraviolet light, but it lets life-giving visible light pass through, and it is high up in the atmosphere exactly where it needs to be to do the job.

The Right Angle

The axis of rotation of the earth is not straight up and down, in relation to the sun, but is tilted at an angle of 23.5 degrees. That is, a line drawn from the south pole of the earth through the north pole is not perpendicular to a line drawn from the sun to the earth. The angle between the axis of rotation of the earth and a line from the sun is 66.5 degrees, or 23.5 degrees less than 90 degrees.

The very existence of that angle, and the exact size of that angle, are both very important. Under the conditions now existing on the earth, we could grow food on only a small part of the earth, if the angle of rotation of the earth was straight up and down. Most of Canada and other countries that are far from the equator—either far to the north or far to the south—would have winter all year long. Large parts of the United States and many other countries would never get warm enough for food to grow. It is only because of the *angle* of rotation of the earth that we have summertime in Canada, and the United States, and other countries, which enable us to grow food in these places. Furthermore, 23.5 degrees is just the right angle to create a perfect difference between summer and winter.

There are many, many other things on the earth that have to be exactly the way they are for life to exist. All *those* things just couldn't happen by accident. That is one reason why many scientists, who don't believe the Bible, still believe in creation.

24

The Earth's Neighbors

The earth is not the only planet in the Solar System. The Solar System consists of the sun and nine planets—Mercury, Venus, Earth, Mars, Jupiter, Saturn, Uranus, Neptune, and Pluto. There are also at least 60 moons in the Solar System (there may be others that we haven't yet discovered). The earth has one moon, Mars has two, Jupiter has 16, Saturn has 18, Uranus has 15, Neptune has eight, and Pluto has one. The Solar System also contains a variety of asteroids and comets.

Halley's Comet

The Solar System is like a big machine—very complex and orderly. The positions of the planets and their orbits around the sun can be known *exactly*. Even the orbit of a comet around the sun can be accurately calculated. Astronomers can tell, *exactly*, the next time a particular comet will appear. Thus, astrono-

Saturn

mers knew that Halley's Comet would appear in 1910 and that it would be seen again 75 years later, in 1985, and that it will be seen again in 2060. Astronomers can tell us, to the exact minute—on any particular day of the year—when the sun will rise, and when it will set. They can tell us when the tide will be highest, and when it will be lowest—on any day of the year—at any point on the earth.

Jupiter and Moons

It is reasonable to assume, then, that intelligent calculations about the Solar System can be projected and realized, because it was designed by One who is intelligent, orderly, and dependable.

PLANTS AND FLOWERS, AND MANY OTHER BEAUTIFUL THINGS

The Creation of Plants

And God said, Let the earth bring forth grass, the herb yielding seed, and the fruit tree yielding fruit after his kind, whose seed is in itself, upon the earth: And it was so.

And the earth brought forth grass, and herb yielding seed after his kind, and the tree yielding fruit, whose seed was in itself, after his kind: And God saw that it was good.

And the evening and the morning were the third day.

Genesis 1:11-13.

Y ou will notice that God made plants on the third day, but He didn't make the sun until the fourth day. If plants get life-giving energy from the light of the sun, how could they

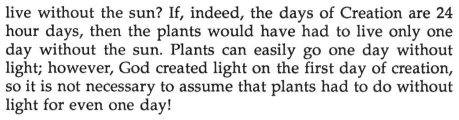

live without the sun? If, indeed, the days of Creation are 24 hour days, then the plants would have had to live only one day without the sun. Plants can easily go one day without light; however, God created light on the first day of creation, so it is not necessary to assume that plants had to do without light for even one day!

You will notice the Bible says that God called forth grass, plants, and trees, and commanded that each should reproduce after its kind. He certainly didn't command that grass or some simple things should come forth first, and then that these things should slowly, over million of years, change into plants, which, over many, many more millions of years should evolve into pine trees, and things like that, which then were to slowly evolve over many, many more millions of years into fruit trees. No, the Bible says that God made grass as grass, plants as plants, and trees as trees, right from the start.

Plants are very, very important to all other living things on the earth. No life would be possible without plants. However, almost all energy used here for life on the earth comes from the sun. You and I, however, cannot capture and use that energy. If we lie in the sun all day, what happens? We get sun-burned! But what about all the green plants around us? They absorb energy from the sun and use it, and, of course, we use the plants for *our* energy!

Photosynthesis

There is one big reason why plants can use energy directly from the sun and why we can't. They have a marvelous apparatus for doing that, - called *photosynthesis*. Photosynthesis is extremely complicated. There are many very large and complex molecules that are involved in photosynthesis, and everything has to be arranged in just a certain way for photosynthesis to work. Many thousands of scientists have been doing research on photosynthesis for many years, and yet there is much about it that we don't understand.

Not only is photosynthesis very, very complicated, *it had to be in place from the very beginning!*

If all of life is dependent on energy that comes from the sun, and photosynthesis is the machinery that captures that energy and converts it into the kind of energy (chemical energy) that can be used by living things, then there could be no life on the earth without photosynthesis, or at least not without some sort of equally complex machinery. If photosynthesis requires complicated machinery right from the start, it is obvious that it could not have slowly and gradually evolved over millions of years, because there would not have been the mechanism to fuel the machinery necessary to energize the mechanism!

The Unchangeable Laws of Science

There are two immutable laws of biology on this earth. That is, there are two laws about life that never change. These two laws are: One, life can only come from life; and two, that *like* always gives rise to *like*. Flies don't erupt magically from rotting food, frogs don't suddenly spring to life from swamps, and dirty rags don't give birth to rats, but this is what many people used to believe. Even after it was proven that flies, frogs, rats, and such, come only from parent flies, frogs, and rats, many people still believed that tiny, microscopic forms of life, like bacteria, suddenly came to life from dead matter. They saw algae, for example, begin to appear on the surface of broth, and thought it somehow spontaneously appeared. It was Louis Pasteur, the famous French scientist, who was a Christian, and who believed in creation, who proved that even tiny microscopic creatures like algae, amoeba, and bacteria come from *preexisting* forms of life.

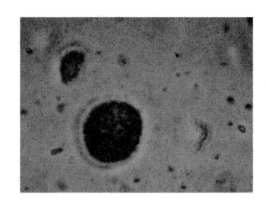

Algae (*Volvox*)

The other law we mentioned, that "*like* always gives rise to *like*," is also very obviously true. Fruit flies always give rise to fruit flies; penguins always give birth to baby penguins; humans always have babies that are human.

The Bible tells us that life came from preexisting life—that God, a living Being, is the the One who created life. The Bible also tells us that God commanded each living thing to reproduce after its own kind. Thus, Genesis teaches exactly what has come to be recognized as these immutable laws of the science of biology.

"Like always gives rise to like."

On the other hand, evolution requires that one believe that somehow, at some time on this earth, life arose from dead, inorganic matter—that life came from a non-living world. It also requires a belief that the immutable law of "*like* always

29

gives rise to *like*," was somehow suspended, temporarily, so that reptiles gave rise to birds, and some non-flying animal gave rise to the bat, and apes gave rise to human beings.

When one proposes that a theory is *scientific*, whether it be the theory of evolution or the theory of creation, one must test that theory against the known laws of science. A creation scientist has found that the theory of creation stands the test of the immutable laws of science, and that what he discovers in the world around him continually bears out the truth of what he reads in the Word of God. Evolutionists, on the other hand, have to imagine things that are *against* science. Thus, evolution might best be called a system of belief, or a "religion," which requires its followers to deny the necessity of God, at the cost of their scientific integrity. It is actually pseudoscience, or false science.

The Incredible Complexity of Life

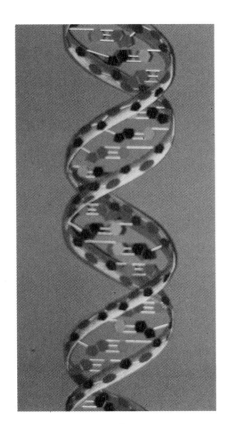

DNA

As we have mentioned, photosynthesis is extremely complicated, and it exists for a very, very important reason. Using photosynthesis, green plants trap the light energy from the sun and convert it into chemical energy. Using the chemical energy so produced, plants take very simple substances like water, carbon-dioxide, ammonia, phosphorus, sulfur, and other simple chemicals and build them into very complicated things, such as starches, proteins, DNA, and RNA—things required for life and growth. A green plant must also have a lot of other very complicated machinery, in order to be able to manufacture starches and proteins. Furthermore, in order to reproduce itself, a plant must be able to produce seeds. That really requires a lot of complicated machinery, and in order to make an exact copy—that is, to produce "after its kind "—that machinery has to be very, very complicated, and has to be able to work very reliably.

Even the simplest living thing known to science—a bacterium—is very complex. In fact, there is no such thing as a "simple form of life." The least complicated form of life that scientists have discovered is still extremely complex. This "very simple form of life" (an organism with only a single cell, like a bacterium), must have a membrane all around it. Membranes not only act like a wall to keep cells together, they also allow only particular kinds of molecules to come into the cell, and only particular kinds of molecules to pass out of the cell. Even this tiniest form of life, invisible to the naked eye, exhibits detail of design and function.

Inside a cell—even the "simplest" cell imaginable—there is very complex machinery. Machinery must exist to synthesize (that is, to manufacture) proteins, DNA, and RNA (and the machinery that does this consists of proteins, DNA, and RNA!). There must be machinery in every single cell (like photosynthesis, for example) to generate the energy that the cell must have. Every cell must have the ability to reproduce itself, exactly. To reproduce itself, the "simplest" cell has to have hundreds of different kinds of proteins, and hundreds—and perhaps even thousands—of different kinds of DNA and RNA molecules. Furthermore, all of these things must be arranged in precise fashion for life to exist, just as everything in an automobile factory must be arranged in assembly lines for these factories to produce automobiles, and everything in a watch must be in precise order for the watch to run.

The Apollo 17 spacecraft as complicated as it is, is very simple compared to a living cell.

American astronauts have walked on the moon, but before we could accomplish this astounding feat, many thousands of scientists, mathematicians, and engineers had to work very hard for many, many years. A lot of intelligent people had to do a lot of research—a lot of planning, a lot of designing—much, much work. All kinds of very complicated machines were built and tested. The spacecraft that flew the astronauts to the moon had millions of parts. Why were we successful in landing astronauts on the moon? We succeeded in landing astronauts on the moon because *absolutely nothing was left to chance.*

However, the *simplest* living thing imaginable would have to be *vastly* more complicated than the spacecraft that was used to put our astronauts on the moon. In fact, when it comes to design and function, there is just no comparison between a living cell and a spacecraft. A spacecraft, as complicated as it is, is very simple, compared to a living cell.

The Origin of Life

How, then, do evolutionists believe that life came into existence? Why, just by chance! Evolution teaches that no

31

one did any planning; nothing was designed; no one did any research, and that no intelligence was involved. Everything that was necessary to put together the vast number of chemical processes in just the precise way to produce life just happened by accident! This takes a giant leap of faith on the part of the evolutionist, but it is not a *reasonable* faith.

A story of great faith is found in the Bible. One day a Roman centurion asked Jesus to heal his servant who was very sick (Matthew 8:5-13). Jesus said that He would go to the centurion's house and heal the servant. The centurion said that wouldn't be necessary, because he believed that all Jesus had to do was "speak the word only," and his servant would be healed. Jesus said that the centurion had marvelous faith—greater than He had ever seen anywhere, and Jesus healed the servant.

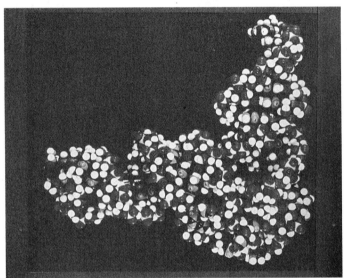

Protein molecule

That centurion had reasonable faith, based upon the fact that he recognized that the One who has created all living systems has supreme power over all life. Evolutionists must have faith, as well, but their belief that something as wonderfully designed, as incredibly complicated, and as intricately coordinated as a living cell could just put itself together, is not reasonable. It is forced upon them because they choose *not to believe* that the great Master Engineer of the universe—God, Himself—created life, just as we read in the Bible.

Furthermore, to believe that life created itself requires not only blind faith, but also, it demands poor science, or what is called pseudo, or false science. It can be shown, using scientific methods, that it is *impossible* for life to have created itself, even if given 4.6 billion years (the age of the earth claimed by many evolutionists).

In truth, the origin of life would require hundreds of different kinds of protein molecules, and hundreds—most likely thousands—of different kinds of DNA (deoxyribonucleic acid) molecules and RNA (ribonucleic acid) molecules. Furthermore, because there are 350 million cubic miles of water on earth, and presumably all life-building chemicals would be dissolved in the water, one would have to have many billions of tons, each, of every protein, DNA, and RNA molecule, in order to produce the simplest form of life.

Each protein, each DNA, and each RNA molecule is very large and complex. Let us consider the probability of the production of one single protein molecule, by chance. Proteins are long chains, and the links in the chains are called *amino acids*. There are 20 different *kinds* of amino acids in proteins. In order to make a particular protein, (for instance, growth hormone), or hemoglobin (the red blood protein that helps red blood cells carry oxygen), the amino acids in each protein have to be arranged in precise order. The average protein has 400 amino acids (actually 20 *different* kinds) in it, although some have over 2,000 amino acids, and a few have less than 100, but never less than 50.

In order to make it easier to calculate, instead of a protein with 400 amino acids in it, let us calculate the probability of producing (by chance) a protein with only 100 amino acids in it. In order to help you understand the laws of probability, let us think for a moment about another problem: If 17 people were asked to line up in a certain order, then rearrange themselves in a different order, then do it again, and again, and . . . How many times could they line up without lining up twice in the same order? Perhaps 1,000 times? Maybe a million times? The truth is, these 17 people could line up over *355 trillion times* without lining up twice in the same order! (That answer is obtained by multiplying 1x2x3x4x5x6x7x. . . x17 times each other). If I wrote down the names of 17 people on a piece of paper, and they didn't know what the order was, they would have only one chance out of 355 trillion of lining up in the right order—and if only one more person is added, for a total of 18 people, they would have only one chance out of six quadrillion, 390 trillion (18x355 trillion) of lining up in the right order!

In the above example, we are talking about the chances of lining up only 17 or 18 things in a certain order by chance, but in a protein, with 100 amino acids, you have to line up **100** things in precise order! In this case, however, since there are only 20 different *kinds* of amino acids, the answer is obtained by multiplying 1/20 times itself 100 times. The answer turns out to be ONE chance out of 10,000,000,000,000,000,000,000, 000,000,000,000,000,000,000,000,000,000,000,000,000,000,000, 000,000,000,000,000,000,000,000,000,000,000,000,000,000,000, 000,000!

Or, one chance out of the number one followed by 130 zeroes or, flatly, zero! But if, by some miracle, the amino acids lined up, what would this produce? One single molecule of

The possibility of amino acids randomly forming into protein = 0 one single protein! However, to have even the remotest chance of getting life started, *billions of tons* each of *hundreds* of different kinds of proteins, and *billions of tons* each of *hundreds* of DNA and RNA molecules must be produced and, of course, the probability of that happening by chance, through evolution, is absolutely zero!

DNA and RNA molecules are even more complex than proteins. Just recently, it has been discovered that the DNA molecule—the gene that codes for only one of the many proteins involved in blood clotting—has 186,000 links (these links are called nucleotides) in its chain. If only *one* of those 186,000 nucleotides is wrong, the body cannot manufacture that blood-clotting factor, and the person suffers from hemophilia.

Moreover, a living cell is not just a bag of protein, DNA, RNA, and other kinds of molecules, a living cell has membranes, energy factories, protein factories, a reproductive information center, and much more, and all of this has to function in just a certain way. Evolution teaches that this would all have to happen by chance.

As mentioned in Chapter 2, Sir Fred Hoyle is one of the world's most famous astronomers. For most of his life, he did not believe in God or creation. A few years ago, he and a friend of his, Professor Chandra Wickramasinghe, also a well-known astronomer, and an evolutionist who was also an atheist, became interested in the problem of the origin of life. Assuming that the earth was five billion years old, they calculated the probability of life evolving on the earth sometime during that five billion years. The probability turned out to be one chance out of the number *one* followed by 40,000 zeroes. Of course, that meant that there was no possibility at all, so they turned to outer space, and conjectured that there are possibly 100 billion galaxies in the universe, and perhaps 100 billion stars in each galaxy. They made the assumption that every star in the universe had a planet like the earth, and that the universe is 20 billion years old, and *THEN* calculated the probability that life evolved somewhere.

For evolutionists, the answer was grim. The chances were so low that, for all practical purposes, there was no probability that life had evolved anywhere in the entire universe. Sir Fred

Hoyle said that the probability of evolution is equal to the probability that a tornado, sweeping through a junkyard, would assemble a Boeing 747! Sir Fred Hoyle and Professor Wickramasinghe are no longer atheists. They say that wherever life exists in the universe, it had to be created! Therefore, *THERE MUST BE A GOD!*

The idea that life evolved, is false. People believe it only because they *don't want* to believe that God created life. But today, on the basis of science alone, the only explanation for the origin of life is still, "In the beginning, God created . . . ."

Why Diseases?

God gave us a world that is beautiful and green.

If God created everything, including bacteria, and He looked on everything He had created and said that it was "very good" (Genesis 1:31), then why do some bacteria cause diseases that make people get sick and die? How could God say that such things are very good? The answer to "why diseases," is found in the third chapter of Genesis. God created a perfect universe, with no disease, no pain, no suffering, and no death. Then man disobeyed God, and sinned. Because of man's sin and rebellion against God, death came into the world, and subsequently, pain, suffering, catastrophes, and disease. When this happened, some bacteria and other microscopic creatures turned into disease germs. They weren't created that way, but God let them decay into disease-causing germs, as a result of His curse on creation.

As you know, most plants are green, so we live in a world that is beautiful, and green. God had a purpose in that, too. Green is the color that is most pleasant to the eyes. Many years ago, all the special clothes that were worn by doctors and nurses in operating rooms were white. It was finally discovered that green was a lot easier on the eyes than white (or any other color), and that by switching from white to green, it would help relieve the eye strain that doctors and nurses suffered from during long operations. Scientists at last discovered what God has always known—that green is the color that is best for our eyes.

Fruits and Flowers

If evolution is true, then "simple" plants, like mosses, evolved slowly, and gradually changed into plants that have seeds, and the seed-bearing plants then evolved into plants and trees that have flowers. This is what evolutionists believe must have happened, because, they say, plants, such as mosses, are more "simple" than ordinary seed-bearing plants, and these seed-bearing plants are more "simple" than plants that have flowers. If this is true, then scientists who study fossils (paleontologists), should have discovered many fossils of plants that were changing from seed-bearing plants into flowering plants. Natural history museums should have many thousands of such in-between kinds (called transitional forms, or intermediate kinds), if evolution is really true. Just as we would expect on the basis of creation, however, fossil hunters have not been able to find these in-between kinds, or transitional forms. Right from the start, mosses always have been mosses; seed-bearing plants, like pine trees, always have been seed-bearing plants, and flowering plants, like roses and apple trees, always have been flowering plants.

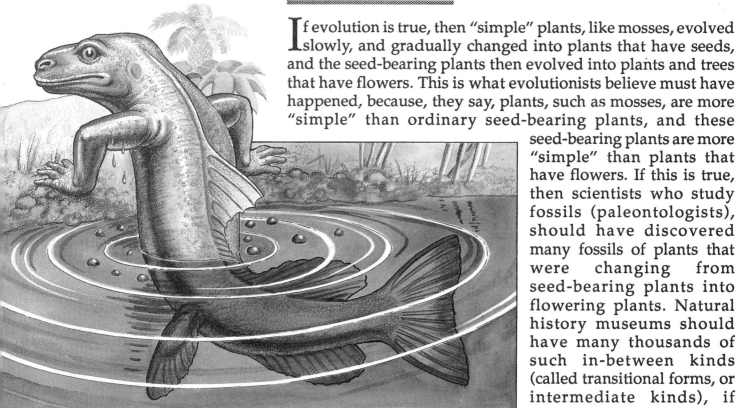

Non-existent transitional form from fish to amphibian

This is true of each one of the many different kinds of plants. Dr. E. J. H. Corner is a botanist at Cambridge University, in England. He is an expert on plants and plant fossils. He is an evolutionist, but in a book published in 1961, Dr. Corner said he still believed that to any fair-minded person, the fossil record of plants was in favor of creation—not evolution. You may wonder, then, why Dr. Corner is an evolutionist instead of a creationist. Since Dr. Corner is a botanist, he knows more about plants than anything else in science. If the fossil record of plants points to creation instead of evolution, as Dr. Corner admits is true, then one would think Dr. Corner would believe in creation. The truth is that many scientists believe in evolution, not because the scientific evidence favors evolution instead of creation, but because they *prefer* to believe in evolution, no matter what the scientific evidence says. If one believes in creation, then one has to believe in a Creator.

Our world is full of an endless variety of beautiful flowers. Flowers are some of the most wonderful things that God has created, but evolutionists believe flowers just happened. They theorize that flowers evolved, in order to attract bees and other insects that help to fertilize these plants, but cannot answer the question of why such a great variety of flowers would evolve to attract insects, when just a few would do the job. It seems evident, to a creationist, that the tremendous variety of flowers on this earth, with all the colors of the rainbow, must have been created by God, mainly for the pleasure of men and women whom He also created.

Also, what about all those wonderful peach, apricot, apple, plum, pear, and orange trees? Why would trees bear all that wonderfully delicious fruit if it weren't for the benefit of people and animals? If people or animals do not eat the fruit, it just drops to the ground and rots. Again, it seems completely unreasonable to believe that the tremendous variety of fruit trees we have on the earth simply evolved by accident, with no purpose for the fruit other than to help the tree that produces it. It is reasonable to believe that God made fruit trees for their scent, in time of blossom, and so that the fruit would serve as food for humans and animals, just as the Bible tells us (Genesis 1:29,30).

The facts of science tell us that life could not evolve by accident or by any sort of imaginary evolutionary process, whatsoever, but that God is the Master Chemical Engineer. The amazing complexity of even the "simplest" plant, and then the incredible variety of plants on the earth—the softness and pleasantness of green, the major color with which God blankets the earth—the endless variety of beautiful flowers, and the many kinds of delicious fruits that provide both pleasure-giving and life-giving food for people and animals, all show the wonder of the third day of Creation Week. "And God saw that it was good" (Genesis 1:12).

Chapter **4**

LIFE IN THE SEA—
THE CREATION OF FISHES,
WHALES, AND MANY OTHER THINGS

And God said, Let the waters bring forth abundantly the moving creature that hath life, and fowl that may fly above the earth in the open firmament of heaven.

And God created great whales, and every living creature that moveth, which the waters brought forth abundantly, after their kind, and every winged fowl after his kind: and God saw that it was good.

And God blessed them, saying, Be fruitful, and multiply, and fill the waters in the seas, and let fowl multiply in the earth.

And the evening and the morning were the fifth day.

Genesis 1:20-23.

Invertebrates

All kinds of creatures live in the sea—some of the smallest and some of the largest, some that are very beautiful, and some that are bizarre, or odd. The smallest creatures that live in the sea are tiny, microscopic, single-celled forms of life, such as bacteria, protozoa, and algae. Not all algae are tiny, however, although many have only a single cell. Seaweeds, which grow to be many feet in length, are algae. Sea dwellers also include many kinds of complex invertebrates, such as sponges, jellyfish, clams, oysters, sea urchins, sea cucumbers, starfish, sea lilies, brachiopods, trilobites (now believed to be extinct), lobsters, worms, snails, barnacles, and others. Many billions times billions of each of these creatures exist in the seas today. Some are simply soft-bodied, like worms and jellyfish, while others, such as clams, oysters, and brachiopods, have shells on the outside, and soft inner parts. Others, such as lobsters and the now-presumed-extinct trilobites, have a tough external outer covering, called an exoskeleton, with soft inner parts. All of these creatures are very, very complicated, with specialized organs for digestion, reproduction, and locomotion.

Vertebrates

Of course, we all know about the many different kinds of fish that live in the seas, lakes, and streams. They, too, are numerous. It has been estimated that there are a billion billion herring in the seas today. Fish, like amphibians, reptiles, and mammals, have an internal skeleton, and are thus said to be vertebrates. There are also mammals that live in the sea. These include whales, dolphins, porpoises, seals, sea lions, and sea cows. Mammals include those creatures that are warm-blooded, give birth to their babies alive, and suckle their young. Long ago there were also marine reptiles (called "sea monsters" in legend and folklore), such as plesiosaurs and ichthyosaurs, that lived in the seas. Apparently they and the dinosaurs became extinct, due to many of the same environmental conditions.

In Chapter 3, it was mentioned that even tiny, microscopic, single-celled forms of life, such as bacteria, are extremely complex. In fact, life is so infinitely complex, if scientists could study bacteria and other such forms of life *forever*, there would no doubt still be much we would never understand. Of course, the many invertebrates and vertebrates that live in the sea and on the land are much more complicated than bacteria. They have very complex nervous systems, digestive systems, reproductive systems, circulatory systems (systems for circulating blood), and sense organs (for seeing, hearing, smelling, and touching).

Where did all of these marvelous creatures come from? How can we account for the existence of such a tremendous variety of creatures? The Bible tells us that these creatures were created by God, according to His own desire. By His unlimited knowledge, wisdom, and power, He conceived, designed, engineered, and made all of these creatures. As we have described earlier, however, evolutionists believe that life created itself. That is, the first tiny microscopic form of life was the result of chance processes due to chemistry and physics. Evolution teaches that the first tiny, one-celled form of life somehow evolved into or produced every other form of life that now exists or that has ever existed on the earth. Evolution says man has had a common ancestor with apes, snakes, cockroaches, onions, bacteria, and every other living thing on the earth, and that you and I are here today as the result of millions of DNA accidents!.

How do evolutionists believe this happened? What do they believe could have changed a microscopic single-celled creature into an animal with a brain, eyes, ears, nose, and many other complicated structures? How could such a tiny, one-celled creature evolve into a beautiful flower, such as a rose, or turn into a marvelous plant such as a peach tree? According to the theory of evolution, there was no purpose, no design, no intelligence, whatsoever, involved in this process. All the changes that had to take place to convert that first form of life into all other living creatures were due to accidents, or genetic mistakes.

Genes and Chromosomes

In the nucleus of every one of our trillions of cells is found the genetic material that helps to determine what we are (humans) and what particular characteristics (eye color, skin color, height, intelligence, sex, etc.) we will possess. We received half of this genetic material from each parent. This genetic material, that helps to determine each characteristic, is called a gene, and many thousands of genes are organized into each chromosome. Humans have 46 chromosomes, 23 of which come from each parent. When living things reproduce, whether they are bacteria, pine trees, or humans, copies of all that genetic material must be produced and passed on to each offspring.

The kind of substance of which genes are composed is deoxyribonucleic acid (DNA). As described earlier, each gene, or DNA molecule, is made up of a long chain of many thousands of subunits, or links. We biochemists call these links, or subunits, nucleotides. It is helpful to think of these nucleotides as being the letters of the genetic alphabet. Just as the 26 letters of the English alphabet have been combined in a certain precise order to make up this sentence, so, also, the nucleotides of the genetic alphabet are combined in a certain way to construct the genetic information found in every cell of each form of life.

Theoretical evolutionary flow chart

41

Many copies of this book have been printed. To do so, the precise order of the letters in each sentence had to be reproduced—each sentence, each paragraph, and each chapter had to be arranged in a particular way, so that everything made sense.

When living things reproduce, they must make copies of their many thousands of genes (humans have at least 100,000 genes, and perhaps even a million or more). To do that, many millions, and even billions, of nucleotides must be arranged in the precise order found in the genes. It is utterly incredible how accurately this is done by each living creature.

Mutations

When a typist types a letter, or manuscript, she or he will usually make a number of mistakes—the number depending on the skill and care of the typist. Most of these mistakes are detected and corrected. Many, many thousands of each particular living creature, on the other hand, may reproduce themselves without making a single error in all the billions of nucleotides they had to arrange in precise order. Of course, no creature has to think when he does that—it is all done automatically by the reproductive cells. Once in awhile, however, a mistake is made when a creature reproduces its genes.

Earlier in this book, it was mentioned that there is a gene that codes for blood-clotting factor VIII. The particular sequence or arrangement of the 186,000 nucleotides in that gene tells the cell how to make that blood-clotting factor (blood-clotting factor VIII is a protein of about 2,400 amino acids). Without this blood-clotting factor, the blood clots very poorly, and that person will suffer from a blood defect called hemophilia ("hemo" meaning blood). If, in reproducing that gene, the reproductive cells put in just *one* wrong nucleotide among all those 186,000 nucleotides, and a future offspring inherits that gene, that child will not be able to produce blood-clotting factor VIII and he or she will be a hemophiliac.

These changes, or mistakes that happen when genes are reproduced, are called mutations. In humans, we know that about 2,000 genetic diseases, such as sickle-cell anemia, are caused by mutations. Other mutations cause blindness, sterility (unable to produce offspring), or some other crippling condition. There is no doubt about it! Mutations are bad! In

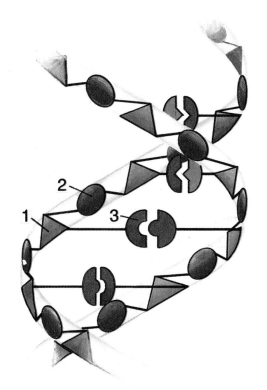

Nucleotides are made up of three parts:
1. Phosphate
2. Sugar
3. Base of Cytosine, Thymine, Adenine, or Guanine.

42

many cases, the mutation is lethal; that is, the creature that inherits the mutation is either born dead or dies sometime soon after birth. As far as I have been able to determine from my studies, all mutations, without exception, are bad!

The Theory of Evolution

Evolutionists say most mutations are bad, but they also believe that once in awhile—maybe once in 10,000—a mutation just happens to be *good*. Just by accident, they say, once in a great while a mutation produces a change in a plant or animal that is good. That is, the creature that inherits the gene with the *good mutation* is changed in such a way that it has gained some advantage, compared to the original creature. Perhaps now, they might imagine, it can run faster, fight better, obtain more food, or produce more offspring. According to evolution theory, the creature that inherits the *good mutation* will reproduce in larger numbers than the original, and so, in the struggle for existence, it will eventually, after hundreds or thousands of years, replace the original. This causes only a slight change, and it takes hundreds, perhaps thousands, of these slight changes to convert a creature into a new species. Thus, the supposed origin of a new species, by evolution, would require tens of thousands of years, or perhaps hundreds of thousands of years. To bring about the evolution of an invertebrate into a fish, or a reptile into a bird, would require perhaps 100 million years or more.

Evolutionists believe a microscopic, single-celled creature evolved into complex invertebrates, such as sponges, jellyfish, and clams. One of these species of invertebrates later gradually evolved into the many kinds of fishes; and still later, some fish evolved into amphibians (a creature that is able to live *both* on land and in the water, such as a salamander). Evolution teaches that amphibians then evolved into reptiles (such as lizards); reptiles evolved into lower mammals (such as moles and shrews); lower mammals evolved into higher mammals (such as apes); and apes finally evolved into humans, which evolution considers the highest mammal of all. Mutation is the commonly accepted mechanism required, by evolution, to change the first form of life into all other living creatures. There is no doubt that all mutations are accidents, or mistakes. The question is, how could harmful mutations ever produce stronger, new species? Evolutionists continue to believe, however, that we are here today as a result of millions of such DNA accidents, or mistakes.

A gene mutation caused this rooster to be born without feathers. He is easily sunburned, unable to regulate body temperature, is constantly attacked by mosquitoes and is unable to mate because of his lack of feathers to flap his wings.

43

Could God Have Used Evolution?

There are some people, called *theistic evolutionists*, who believe that God used evolution to create everything on the earth today. But evolution is the most wasteful, inefficient, cruel method that could ever be devised to create living things. Even evolutionists admit that almost all mutations are bad—causing cripples, sickness, disfigurements, and deaths. Even the so-called "good" mutants, evolutionists believe, must enter into a struggle for existence, and only survive because they are able to outcompete and eliminate the original. This process, evolutionists declare, produced every living creature in existence today, starting about four billion years ago with a single, microscopic form of life.

God is all-powerful and all-wise. Why would He use such a wasteful, inefficient, cruel method to create man, taking three billion years to do it, when He is able to create instantaneously? The answer is—He didn't! There isn't the slightest hint, anywhere in the Bible, that God used evolution, and there is not one fact of science which proves that God used evolution to create anything.

Invertebrates — No Evolution!

As we have described above, evolutionists believe that life started with a tiny, microscopic, single-celled form of life, perhaps similar to a bacterium. They believe this tiny form of life evolved into complex, multicellular forms of life, such as jellyfish, sponges, clams, lobsters, trilobites, starfishes, etc. Scientific reports have been published about the discovery of fossils of bacteria and algae in rocks said to be three to three-and-a-half billion years old. In Cambrian rocks, believed by evolutionists to have formed 600 million years ago, are found vast numbers of *fossils* of invertebrates, such as sponges, trilobites, jellyfish, sea cucumbers, brachiopods, and other kinds of highly complex invertebrates. Thus, if evolutionists are correct, these Cambrian animals appeared on Earth about two-and-one-half *billion years* after the first microscopic form of life evolved.

Therefore, according to evolutionists' beliefs, we have rocks three billion years old containing fossils of microscopic, single-celled creatures, and rocks about 600 million years old, containing fossils of a great variety of highly complex invertebrates that had evolved from these single-celled forms of life. In between, according to evolutionists, are rocks that are supposed to date from three billion years old to about 600 million years old. These rocks are called Precambrian rocks. Sometimes these rocks are several thousand feet thick. Many are undisturbed, and are perfectly suitable for the preservation of fossils. If evolution is true, then in these rocks we should find fossils of many transitional forms, or intermediates, between the microscopic, single-celled creatures and the vast multitude of complex invertebrates. Surely, since paleontologists have found fossils of microscopic, soft-bodied, single-celled bacteria, they should be able to find fossils of everything between those creatures and the complex invertebrates.

The truth is, not one single fossil intermediate or transitional form, between the microscopic single-celled creatures and the complex invertebrates, has ever been found! When they first appear in the fossil record, jellyfish are jellyfish; sea urchins are sea urchins; sponges are sponges; and trilobites are trilobites; and that is true of all other invertebrates. There is not one shred of scientific evidence to indicate that these many different kinds of invertebrates ever evolved. In fact, creation scientists ask, what greater evidence for creation could the rocks give than the abrupt appearance of this great variety of very complex creatures, without a trace of earlier, intermediate forms? This is powerful, positive evidence for creation. This fact alone—this huge gap between microscopic, single-celled creatures and the complex, multicellular animals—proves, beyond doubt, that evolution *has not* taken place.

Excavation of fossil bed at Dinosaur National Monument.

Fossil graveyard

And Then—All at Once — Fishes!

Evolutionists believe that over a period of 100 million years, one or more of the invertebrates evolved into fishes, which they believe were the first vertebrates. Evolutionists can't agree as to whether a worm, or a sea urchin, or a sponge evolved into a fish—and not one single fossil intermediate between an invertebrate and a fish has ever been found! If an invertebrate evolved into a fish over 100 million years, billions of the intermediates must have lived and died during that vast stretch of time. Our museums ought to contain many thousands of fossil transitional forms.

45

Vast numbers of the fossil *invertebrates* have been found; vast numbers of fossil *fish* have been found. But absolutely nothing, in between, has ever been found! The fossil evidence shows that every one of the many different *kinds* of fishes appear fully formed, and distinct.

Sea Mammals

Most mammals, including humans, horses, cows, dogs, rats, apes, monkeys, elephants, pigs, tigers, and camels, live on land. However, some mammals live in the sea—whales, dolphins, porpoises, seals, sea lions, and sea cows. Evolutionists believe that these "marine mammals" evolved from mammals that used to live on the land. Some believe that many millions of years ago, a hairy, four-legged mammal ventured into the water in search of food, or sanctuary. The tail gradually changed into flukes; the hind legs slowly disappeared; the front legs changed into flippers; and finally, over eons of time, these creatures became what we know today as the whale. One evolutionist suggested that the ancestor of whales and dolphins may have resembled a cow, a pig, or a buffalo.

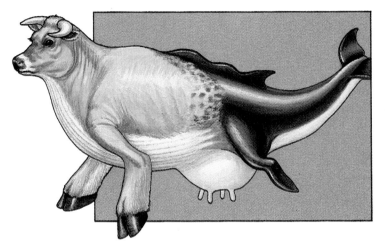

Transitional forms would have been extremely vulnerable in either of the worlds they theoretically were bridging.

Let us suppose that the ancestor of the whale was a cow, and for some reason, this cow ventured into the ocean. For some strange reason, her tail started to evolve into the broad flukes of a whale (maybe it was no longer needed to switch flies, since she was in the water). That is, genetic mistakes, or mutations, *just happened* to gradually change her tail into flukes. Other genetic accidents caused her hind legs to start to get smaller and smaller. Another strange thing began to happen—genetic mistakes started to change her front legs into flippers. And very, very strangely, her nostrils began to move from the end of her snout towards the top of her head.

Let us stop to consider what this creature would look like halfway through this *evolution*. Her tail is only partway flukes. It is no longer good for switching flies when she goes ashore, which she must do, often, because she is only part whale, and still has to spend much of her time on land, and it is not much help yet for swimming. Her hind legs are surely a great embarrassment. They are getting shorter and shorter. Her front legs are surely a mess, too. They are halfway between ordinary

46

feet, and legs, and flippers. This poor thing is at a tremendous disadvantage, while on land. She can't walk, or if she can, it would be terribly awkward. When she is in the water, she looks awfully silly trying to swim, with those part front feet—part flippers, and with a part tail—part flukes. Where does she have her babies, in the water or on the land? If she has them in the water, how does she keep them from drowning, and how does she nurse them?

The whole idea that some hairy, four-legged mammal ventured into the water and gradually changed into a whale, during millions of years, is absurd. A whale is marvelously designed for life in the water. Mother whales are especially made so that they not only can give birth, but they also can nurse their babies under water. Their nostrils are on top of their heads so they can breathe when they are on the surface of the water. The ears of whales are so specially designed that they not only can hear under water, they also can stand the great pressure when they dive to a depth of 100 feet or more. A creature—part cow and part whale—would have none of these special characteristics, and would be unable to live *either* on the land or in the water. Furthermore, paleontologists cannot find a series of transitional forms in the fossil record between whales and some imaginary, hairy, four-legged ancestor.

The same is true for the marine reptiles, the plesiosaurs, ichthyosaurs, and others. The ichthyosaurs, although they were air-breathing reptiles with internal skeletons, like land-dwelling reptiles, in many ways looked quite fish-like. Evolutionists believe marine reptiles evolved from four-legged reptiles that lived on land. Paleontologists have found many fossils of the plesiosaurs—with paddles instead of feet and legs, and they have found many fossils of the fish-like ichthyosaurs. They also have found many fossils of reptiles that lived on the land, but they have yet to find a single fossil of a part-land, part-marine reptile. Evolutionists believe that it took millions of years for a land reptile to evolve into a marine reptile. If this is true, fossils of transitional forms should have been found in abundance. Their complete absence from the fossil record is contradictory to evolution, thus giving marvelous confirmation of the fact that God created the fish of the seas and whatsoever passes through the paths of the sea.

Ichthyosaurus—
a marine reptile

47

Chapter

ANIMALS FOR THE
LAND AND THE AIR

And God said, Let the earth bring forth the living creature after his kind, cattle, and creeping thing, and beast of the earth after his kind: And it was so.

And God made the beast of the earth after his kind, and cattle after their kind, and everything that creepeth upon the earth after his kind: and God saw that it was good.

Genesis 1:24,25

Genesis 1:31 teaches that all of the above took place on the sixth day of creation. As we read in Genesis 1:20-23, the birds of the air were created on the fifth day. There are many animals that live on the land and fly in the air, and we will study some of the most interesting ones. Dinosaurs are special, because many of them were so large, and so strange, and different from anything living on the earth today. An entire chapter—Chapter 6—will be devoted to the dinosaurs. In this chapter (Chapter 5), we will learn more about amphibians, reptiles, mammals, and birds and the scientific evidence related to their origin.

Amphibians

Evolutionists believe that animal life began in the sea. They believe the first kinds of animals that lived on the land were amphibians. The word "amphibian" is used to refer to something that spends time both on land and in the water. Modern-day amphibians include frogs, toads, newts, and salamanders. These creatures like to live near the water, and the mother lays her eggs in the water, where they hatch to become *larvae* (the early form of an animal, such as a frog).

Metamorphosis of the Frog

We are all familiar with a larval frog, the tadpole. At this stage, the baby frog has gills, like fish, and swims and

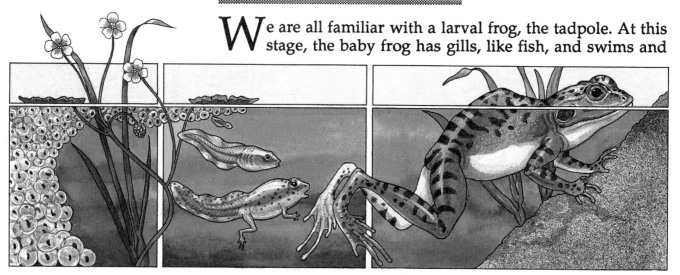

lives in the water. Then, at just the right time, the gills disappear, lungs develop, front and hind feet begin to form, and the tadpole changes into a frog. This process is called *metamorphosis* (a change into a different physical form).

Some people believe that metamorphosis is evidence for evolution—that a swimming tadpole "evolves" into an animal that has legs and spends most of its time on the land. Actually, the process of metamorphosis is an embarrassment to evolutionists. It defies any explanation based on evolution. During metamorphosis, fins do not "evolve" into feet and legs, and gills do not "evolve" into lungs. All of the information or instructions to form the tadpole and the adult frog are present in the fertilized frog egg, and nothing has to accidentally come into existence by mutations. In fact, if a mutation *does* take place in the egg, the tadpole dies, or produces a crippled frog. Let's examine this metamorphosis.

The egg first develops into a tadpole. This tadpole has gills, so it obtains oxygen from the water, just like a fish does. When the tadpole begins to change into a frog, the gills disappear, and the lungs develop from an entirely different place, as do the legs. The lungs and legs do not form or "evolve" from pre-existing gills and fins, but are said to form *de novo*, meaning "from something new" or "from something original."

Evolution is faced with an animal that lives and swims in the water, obtaining oxygen from water through its gills. Then suddenly the old creature disappears and the animal has legs, lives out on the ground much of the time, and has a marvelous set of lungs for breathing air—a creature that wasn't even hinted at in the structure of the tadpole. How does an animal made for life in the water change into an animal that is made to live and breathe *out* of the water, with feet and legs, while at the same time retaining all of its former characteristics? If it has "evolved" into a frog, how does its reproductive genes "remember" how to be a tadpole? How could it "evolve" legs, and at the same time live and swim in the water? Why would it "evolve" lungs, when the gills were doing a perfectly good job of obtaining oxygen from the water? What advantage would it be for a tadpole to start evolving feet and legs? How did everything get perfectly timed so this creature had everything happen just at the right time to make him a tadpole, and then all those other things happen just at the right time to change him into a frog? Metamorphosis is evidence of a complexity of functions that only the infinite Designer could have conceived. The frog has brought forth "after its kind" since the sixth day of creation, and, indeed, God has chosen a fascinating, unique way to accomplish this.

Metamorphosis of Butterflies

Even more incredible is the metamorphosis that takes place in the life of a butterfly. This creature starts out as a fertilized egg, then becomes a caterpillar. The caterpillar forms a cocoon, and inside the cocoon it becomes a jelly-like substance. Out of that "jelly" emerges a beautiful butterfly. It no longer lives by eating leaves, but it flits freely from flower to flower. Soon it mates, lays its eggs, and dies, then the cycle repeats itself.

Developing Monarch pupa.

51

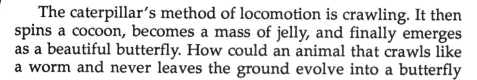

The caterpillar's method of locomotion is crawling. It then spins a cocoon, becomes a mass of jelly, and finally emerges as a beautiful butterfly. How could an animal that crawls like a worm and never leaves the ground evolve into a butterfly

that flies, while at the same time keeping the ability to reproduce another caterpillar? The word "evolution" means "change." In this case, however, the caterpillar does not evolve into a butterfly. The butterfly egg develops first into a perfect caterpillar. Nothing has evolved or changed about the caterpillar. Then, the caterpillar, while remaining a perfect caterpillar, becomes a mass of jelly, which, through some incredible process, develops into a butterfly—a creature that isn't even hinted at in the caterpillar. Evolution is less than inadequate to explain how such an incredible development takes place to produce such a creature one small step at a time, with each intermediate not only managing to survive, but also somehow being superior to the preceding form. And all of that happening as the result of genetic mistakes? In the book, *The Insects* (Time-Life Books, New York, 1962), it is said that "the term metamorphosis has been given to this miraculous change of form in most insects" (p. 56). Later, on that same page, we read, "There is no evidence how such a remarkable plan of life ever came about." Indeed, the change is truly miraculous, and could never be explained as a product of evolution.

Suppose that the caterpillar *did* evolve into a butterfly. The very first problem with which evolution is faced is how does it reproduce? Caterpillars don't lay eggs, or reproduce at all. Evolutionists have to assume that caterpillars, before they became butterflies, *did* reproduce, but in some interim between caterpillar and butterfly, they *lost the ability* to reproduce. The caterpillar decides it would be nice to be beautiful—to have wings and flit about. But one could not imagine a more unlikely candidate for becoming a butterfly!

Even the caterpillar realizes that for him to become a butterfly would call for drastic measures. He has nothing that could evolve into wings; he has mouth parts for chewing up leaves, but he has nothing that could serve as a long tongue for getting nectar out of flowers. Everything about a butterfly is different from a caterpillar. Somehow the caterpillar must develop a method for spinning a cocoon and dissolving into a mass of jelly, so he can start all over again.

What would happen if he never figured out how to change a mass of jelly into a butterfly? Could genetic accidents or mistakes ever change a mass of jelly into a butterfly? The evolutionary scenario could *never* produce a butterfly by changing a caterpillar into a mass of jelly. But God, the Master Engineer of the universe, programmed a mass of jelly to develop into a delicately sculptured butterfly, with everything perfectly designed for a way of life entirely different from that of the caterpillar that dissolved into the jelly.

Origin of Amphibians

From what do evolutionists believe amphibians evolved? Evolutionists believe that fish evolved into amphibians. They believe that more than 400 million years ago, a fish began to crawl out of the water onto land, and gradually evolved into an amphibian. A lot of changes would have to take place in a creature that is designed to spend all of its time in the water, in order to convert it into a creature that spends much of its time on land.

American toad

Fins would have to evolve into feet and legs, such as those possessed by a salamander, for instance. Also, lungs would have to develop, and many other things would have to change.

We need to look for a series of transitional forms in the fossil record which supposedly show fins gradually changing into feet and legs, in order to support evolution. Evolutionists believe a fish evolved into amphibians over millions of years, so it is logical to assume that many billions of those intermediates must have lived and died during those years. Surely scientists ought to be able to find thousands of fossils of the intermediates showing, for example, 95 percent fins, five percent feet and legs, 80 percent fins, 20 percent feet and legs, 50 percent fins, 50 percent feet and legs, and so forth. We have many fossils of the one type of fish that evolutionists believe was the ancestor of amphibians. He was 100 percent fish, with a lovely set of fins designed for balancing, steering, and moving in the water. We have fossils of what evolutionists believe is the oldest amphibian ever discovered. This fossil amphibian does not show part feet, and part legs, and part fins. He has 100 percent feet and legs—the kind of feet and legs found on all such amphibians.

No one has ever found a single fossil of an intermediate with part fins, part feet, and part legs. If evolution is true, scientists ought to be able to find many, many thousands of fossils of the intermediates. But absolutely none have been found!

Frogs are unusual creatures, with very long hind legs especially designed for hopping and leaping. With such an

Fossil fish from Hays State Museum, Hays, Kansas.

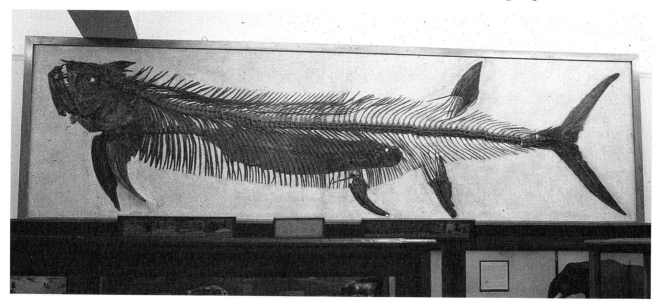

unusual structure, scientists could expect to discover fossils of intermediates, if, indeed, this structure evolved over millions of years, but such intermediates have never been found. The fossil record reveals that frogs have always been frogs. Just as creationists would expect, frogs appear in the fossil record fully formed right at the start, and that is true of all other amphibians.

54

Flying Animals

In this book, we have been looking at the evidence for creation versus the evidence for evolution. When we began to consider the fossil record, we concentrated on those creatures which would offer the best chance of showing evidence for evolution. Now we shall examine the fossil record of the flying animals that should also produce an abundance of evidence

for evolution, if they, too, indeed, did evolve. We know of four different kinds of flying animals: birds, bats (mammals), flying insects, and flying reptiles (which, along with the dinosaurs, became extinct at about the same time).

In each of these cases, evolutionists believe the *flying* animal evolved from a *non-flying* animal. Converting a *non-flying* animal into a *flying* animal requires some very big changes. Thus, the intermediates, if they can be found as fossils, should be easy to recognize as partway between the *non-flying* animal and the *flying* animal. In each case, evolutionists believe, it took millions of years for the *non-flying* animal to evolve into the *flying* animal, and since *four different kinds* of flying animals supposedly evolved, there certainly should be adequate evidence of transitional forms in the fossil record.

Because we lack any fossil evidence to support the evolutionary theory, it is indeed *a leap of faith* to believe the idea of evolution.

Insects

First of all, let's take a look at *flying* insects. Evolutionists are still arguing, among themselves, about what, on a *non-flying* insect evolved into wings. If we could find even one single transitional form, we would be able to know, immediately, what structures on the *non-flying* insect evolved into wings. But not one single transitional form has ever been found!

It is not that scientists cannot find fossils of insects—there are many! Recently, for example, fossils of insects supposedly

Dragonfly

380 million years old have been found. The scientist who found them said they were so perfectly preserved they looked like they had died just yesterday. These fossils included those of spiders, mites, and daddy longlegs. They haven't changed much in that supposed 380 million years!

Not long ago, some fossil cockroaches were discovered. They are also supposed to be 350 million years old, but the scientist who studied them said they looked disgustingly similar to modern cockroaches. She said that cockroaches apparently haven't changed much in 350 million years. What the evolutionist sees as an insect unchanged over millions of years, the creationist sees as an insect not unlike those created on the sixth day of creation, by God.

Many fossils of *flying* insects have also been found. It has been reported that fossils of dragonflies nearly 400 million years old have been found. They are dragonflies! But 400 million years old, they are not! There are many fossils of *non-flying* insects, and there are many fossils of *flying* insects, but there are no fossils of something in between the two. If evolution is true, we ought to have thousands of fossils of intermediate forms. Their total absence is remarkable testimony to the fact of creation.

Flying Reptiles

Flying reptiles were strange creatures, indeed. In Texas paleontologists found fossil remains of a *flying* reptile, *Pteranodon*, with a wingspread of about 52 feet.

Evolutionists believe that *flying* reptiles evolved from *non-flying* reptiles. There were several kinds of *flying* reptiles. *Rhamphorhynchus* was only about one and one-half feet long. He had a long tail with a rudder on the end. The *Pteranodon* had a long, toothless beak; a long bony crest extending backward, and he was very large—as were many of these creatures. All these *flying* reptiles had at least one thing in common—an enormously long fourth finger, which was the main support for the wing membrane.·

What had to happen if these creatures were to have evolved? Many millions of years ago there would have been no such thing as a *flying* reptile—just ordinary reptiles. None of these reptiles ever gave a thought to becoming a *flying* reptile. But (evolution must assume) a genetic accident, or mutation, occurred in one of these reptiles and a little baby reptile hatched that had slightly longer fourth fingers. For some strange, unknown reason (known only to evolution), his slightly longer fourth fingers gave him and his offspring (and all their offspring who happened to inherit the gene for longer fourth fingers) an advantage in the struggle for existence. Thus, in the fight for survival, the reptiles with slightly longer fourth fingers, after many hundreds, and most likely thousands of generations, finally replaced all the *original* reptiles with ordinary fourth fingers.

Rhamphorhynchus. **One of the smaller of the flying reptiles.**

After an unknown time, and no doubt after countless bad mutations had been eliminated, another lucky accident happened—and the fourth fingers got longer again. Another struggle for existence began, and once again, the reptiles with the *longer* fourth fingers replaced all the reptiles with *shorter* fourth fingers. Thus, evolution says, during millions of years and via many, many mutations, the fourth fingers on these reptiles got longer, and longer. And at the same time, other genetic mistakes generated the wing membrane, the flight muscles, caused teeth and jaws to evolve into a long toothless beak (in the case of *Pteranodon*), and caused the bones to become hollow, to make them lighter, for flight.

Imagine one of those reptiles at an intermediate stage. He has only partial wings, so he can't fly. But, on the other hand, he can only walk, very awkwardly, if he can walk at all. In case of the *Pteranodon*, his jaws and teeth are partway toward becoming a toothless beak. Such a creature could not eat properly, or fly, or run around on the ground to catch prey.

Pteranodon and Rhamphorhynchus

57

But evolution teaches that these were the superior forms which gave rise to new species! As one can see, the above scenario is ridiculous! God created flying reptiles, fully formed, able to fly, and to eat, and to reproduce after their kind.

And this is exactly what the fossil record proves. There is not even a trace of a transitional form between *non-flying* and *flying* reptiles. They appear in the fossil record fully formed, and when they disappear from the fossil record, they are the same magnificent creatures.

Bats

Bats are mammals. Thus, like other mammals, they are warm-blooded, have fur, give birth to their babies alive, and the mothers nurse their young. Evolutionists must believe that these *flying* mammals evolved from a *non-flying* mammal,

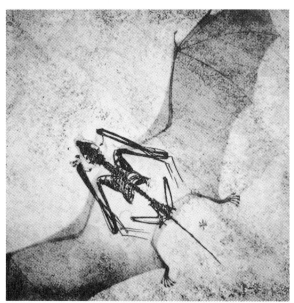

Oldest fossil bat.

similar to a rat, or a squirrel, or tree shrew. Evolution had to accomplish many marvelous things which had to occur in just the right order, so that all of the intermediates could not only survive, but were, in every case, superior to the preceding form.

As in the case of the flying reptiles, a mutation had to lengthen the fingers in order for the bat to evolve. With the bat, however, almost all of the fingers are very long, and support the wing membrane. So, a mutation was necessary that would lengthen almost *all* of the fingers. Evolution teaches struggle for existence—mutation—struggle for existence—mutation...all the while fingers getting longer and longer, and wing membranes and flight muscles developing magically. It was also necessary for these mutations to produce an extremely complicated sonar system, "de novo." That is, there was nothing in the bat's supposed ancestor, from which the sonar system could have evolved. This sonar system is truly marvelous. Although thousands of bats inhabit a particular cave, they are able to fly throughout that cave, in total darkness, without running into each other or banging up against a wall. Each bat sends out a series of very rapid signals which bounce off objects and return to the ear of the bat. From the intensity and direction of these signals that return, the bat can recognize each object within sonar range and fix its exact location. No doubt bats use this system to locate insects when looking for food at night. Even more incredible is the fact that each bat is able to distinguish his own signal from thousands of others. Suppose a person had a thousand radios all around him, each tuned to a different station. It would be impossible to clearly understand any one message. The same would be true with bats, if they did not possess this special ability to recognize their own signal or, as some scientists have suggested, fail to hear all other signals but their own. Although scientists have confirmed that the bat distinguishes his own signal, no one, as yet, has been able to figure out how it's done!

The world's oldest fossil bat is supposed to be 50 million years old. This fossil was discovered in Wyoming, and was studied by Dr. Glenn Jeppsen, a vertibrate paleontologist. This bat is essentially identical to a modern bat. It had the marvelous sonar system just described. He appears in the fossil record without a trace of any earlier ancestors or intermediate forms—a powerful testimony to the fact of creation, and totally contradictory to evolution theory.

Birds

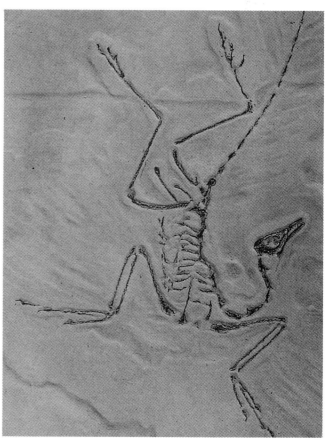

There isn't even the slightest suggestion from the fossil record that *flying insects, flying reptiles,* or *flying mammals* (bats) evolved. One cannot even begin to logically conjecture how these creatures could have evolved slowly and gradually from their supposed ancestors. Still, evolutionists insist there are transitional forms, and often cite a now-extinct animal called *Archaeopteryx* as proof of evolution.

However, the truth is, *Archaeopteryx* was a bird! He had perching feet, the wings of a bird, feathers that were identical to the feathers of modern birds, a bird-like skull, and a furcula (wishbone). Above all that, he flew! Furthermore, although the first fossils of *Archaeopteryx* were discovered about 125 years ago, and other fossils have been found since, not a single transitional form between *Archaeopteryx* and a reptile, or between *Archaeopteryx* and any other bird has ever been found. If reptiles did, indeed, evolve into birds, thousands of intermediate stages

Fossil *Archaeopteryx*

had to have lived and died, thus leaving evidence through their fossil remains.

Despite the weight of evidence to the contrary, many evolutionists maintain that *Archaeopteryx* was a transitional form between *reptile* and *bird*. They point to the fact that this bird had claws on its wings, teeth, and other features that *seem* to be reptile-like. Some might suggest these features indicate that *Archaeopteryx* evolved from a reptile. It is true that modern birds do not have teeth. However, some ancient birds *did* have teeth. By the same token, it is also true many ancient birds *did not* have teeth. The point is, no fossils have ever been found that show a gradual disappearance of teeth in birds. They either had teeth, or they didn't! This is not surprising, because it is also true of all other vertebrates. Some fishes have teeth, some amphibians have teeth, and some reptiles have teeth. But there are fish, and amphibians, and reptiles with *no* teeth! *Most* mammals have teeth, but some *do not*. The presence or absence of teeth neither confirms nor denies evolution or creation.

Archaeopteryx— evolution's supposed reptile-like transitional form.

Are claws on the wings evidence of a transition between reptiles and birds? There are at least three birds living today that have *claws* on the wings. The *hoatzin*, a bird living in South America, has claws on its wing when young. This is also true of the *touraco*, a bird living in Africa. The *ostrich* has three claws on its wings, but no one would dare suggest that any of these birds are *intermediates* between *reptiles* and *birds* because they are very much alive and well today.

A few years ago, a paleontologist found the fossils of a modern bird and concluded, from the evidence, that it had lived at the same time as *Archaeopteryx*. *Archaeopteryx* cannot be the ancestor of birds, if modern birds and *Archaeopteryx* lived at the same time.

More recently, paleontologists found fossils of a bird in Texas that is supposed to have lived 75 million years before *Archaeopteryx*. If evolutionary thinking is followed, this bird should be more *reptile-like* than *Archaeopteryx*. But it is more *bird-like* than *Archaeopteryx*! Creation scientists conclude that *Archaeopteryx* was not an *intermediate* between *reptiles* and *birds*,

60

but was a *bird*, especially created by God and preserved for us in the fossil record.

Mammals from Reptiles?

There are many different kinds of mammals on the earth today—those that *live in the sea* (whales, dolphins, sea cows) and those that *fly* (bats). All mammals are warm-blooded, and mammals, alone among all creatures, produce milk for their young. Most mammals have a covering of hair, or fur, and most all give birth to their babies alive (the spiny anteater and duck-billed platypus lay eggs).

Evolutionists believe that mammals evolved from reptiles. That would require many complex changes, and it seems ridiculous that all of those incredible changes could be brought about in such a way that each creature *intermediate* between the *reptile* and *mammal* not only survived, but was even superior to the animal that preceded it. Evolutionists must somehow believe a *cold-blooded* animal changed into a *warm-blooded* animal. This involves much more than developing a mechanism to warm up the blood. The temperature must also be very carefully regulated. If the body temperature gets too warm, an animal dies; if the body temperature is too cool, an animal is sluggish, and cannot function well. Therefore, if evolution is true, some means had to be invented, by trial and error and chance mutations to regulate body temperature, while at the same time changing the degree of body temperature and adjusting all the systems in the body to operate in accord with that particular temperature. Sensing devices, methods for expanding and contracting blood vessels, sweating, or panting (for cooling purposes), or shivering (for emergencies when cold), had to be developed by blind chance.

Platypus—Australia's confusing mammal.

Consider, also, that the method of reproduction in most all mammals is very different from that of reptiles. *Reptiles lay eggs*, but most *mammalian offspring* are *born alive*. This means the mother must have a very special and complicated means of nourishing and carrying the developing baby until it is born.

The unborn child must also have unique features. Until a baby is born, he does not use his lungs. Therefore, there is no need for blood to circulate to the lungs in order to absorb oxygen from the lungs. Thus the circulatory system of the unborn baby

Otters have special fur that insulates against icy water temperatures.

is so constructed that most of the blood bypasses the lungs. There is a circular muscle at a key location on the large blood vessel that carries the blood as it bypasses the lungs. At birth, this muscle contracts and closes off the bypass, causing the blood to flow through the vessels that go to the lungs. This only happens once in the entire lifetime of the creature! Here is a very special apparatus, vitally necessary for the life of the animal (or human), that functions only once during its entire lifetime. How could the supposed evolutionary process work that out? How could a series of genetic mistakes produce such a delicately balanced event, and how does a mutation anticipate the needs for an apparatus without which the creature dies? Here is undoubted evidence of a brilliant engineering feat produced by the Master Engineer.

> *I will praise Thee; for I am fearfully and wonderfully made: Marvelous are Thy works; and that my soul knoweth right well.*
>
> Psalm 139:14

Mammals have many other special features. They breathe in a way that is very different from the way reptiles breathe. Mammals have a *diaphragm*—a wall composed of muscle and fibrous material that separates the *thorax* (the chest area) from the *stomach area*. Mammals breathe by expanding and contracting the diaphragm. Reptiles do not have a diaphragm, so they cannot breathe that way. They have to use their mouths to draw in and expel air. There is nothing in a reptile from which a diaphragm could have evolved. Therefore, if mammals evolved from reptiles, a diaphragm would have had to develop from nothing.

Further evidence supporting creation is the fact that the ears and the lower jaw of mammals are very different from those of reptiles. In the ears of every mammal, living or fossil, are found three bones, the *incus, malleus* and *stapes*. On each side of the jaw mammals have a single bone, called the *dentary*, because in it the teeth are anchored. In the ears of every reptile, living or fossil, is found a single bone, the *columella*, which corresponds to the *malleus* in the mammal. Every reptile, living or fossil, has *several* bones in the lower jaw. Evolutionists imagine that as the reptile evolved into a mammal, two of those bones somehow were dragged up into the ear, completely refashioned, re-engineered, and refastened in such a way that they produced the marvelous and delicately formed apparatus found in the ears of a mammal. The intermediate forms would still have had to chew, and hear, in order to survive. Even more unbelievable than all of that, is the fact that an essential organ of hearing in all mammals is an incredibly complex structure called the *Organ of Corti*. It also would have had to be invented *de novo*, just as the diaphragm.

Dimetrodon—considered by paleontologists to be a mammal-like reptile.

As incredible as it may seem, evolutionists maintain that mammals evolved from reptiles in spite of all the obvious scientific impossibilities that would have prevented such a transition. Paleontologists have found fossils of creatures they call "mammal-like reptiles." These creatures have some structures found in reptiles and some that are found in mammals. Evolutionists claim that these creatures are intermediates between reptiles and mammals. None of the structures or features found in these creatures is part mammal, part reptile structure, however. In whatever creature they are found, they are complete, *fully functional structures*. Creationists are not surprised to find certain structures, or organs, in two different kinds of animals. After all, a certain structure or feature that is needed in mammals might also be very useful in reptiles. There are a lot of things found in a television that are also found in a radio, but television sets did not evolve from radios.

The Organ of Corti

Peculiar to mammals and the essential organ of hearing (in the middle ear), has 3,000 adjacent arches forming a tunnel. Until complete, or nearly complete, this complicated organ and its supply of hundreds of nerves would be useless.

In summary, *all mammals*, living or fossil, have *three bones* in the ear (and the Organ of Corti!), and a *single bone* on each side of the lower jaw, while each *reptile*, living or fossil, has a *single bone* in the ear and about *six bones* on each side of the lower jaw. No one has ever found a single intermediate with two bones in the ear and two, three, or four bones in the jaw. Furthermore, no one can reasonably explain how the intermediates managed to hear and chew, while all of the necessary restructuring was taking place and the Organ of Corti was being developed. The "mammal-like reptiles" were created as reptiles with certain features also found in mammals, but they were *not* evolutionary intermediates in the process of evolving into mammals.

Horses Were Always Horses

Horses used to be evolutionists' favorite example of their theory. However, this is no longer true. Although I have lectured and debated on most major university campuses in the United States and Canada and in more than 20 foreign countries, I have rarely heard evolutionists mention the fossil record of horses as evidence for evolution. It is now recognized, by most paleontologists, that the fossil record of horses is inconclusive when it comes to evolution, and, therefore, evolutionists no longer want to talk openly about it. Since, however, the "evolution of horses" continues to be used in school textbooks, it is necessary to look at the facts.

Fossil remains of a small animal were first discovered in Europe, and at that time, the animal was given the name *Hyracotherium*, because it so closely resembles a hyrax, or coney. It really looked much more like a hyrax than a horse, but evolutionists needed something to put at the beginning of the family tree of horses, so they adopted the *Hyracotherium* and *renamed* it *Eohippus* ("dawn horse"). Today, many people—even some evolutionists—believe that it wasn't related to horses at all. *Hyracotherium* had four front toes, and three toes on each hind foot. Some fossil remains of horses show they had three toes on their hind feet, while others had three toes with the two outer toes reduced in size, and other horses, including modern horses, had a single toe. Some horses had browsing teeth for eating leaves and tender shoots of trees, as do deer and other browsing animals, while other horses had broad, flat grazing teeth for eating grass.

Even evolutionists acknowledge, however, that we cannot find transitional forms between these various kinds of horses. There are no fossil horses with part-browsing, part-grazing teeth. We cannot find fossils of a horse with three-and-a-half toes or two-and-a-half toes. The fossils show no progressive increase in size. In fact, some "later" horses were smaller than some "earlier" horses. The number of ribs did not progressively increase. The number of ribs in fossil horses go up and down. Just as there are different kinds of primates today—lemurs, monkeys, apes, and humans—so there were different kinds of horses in the past, with no evidence that one kind of horse evolved from another kind of horse. Just as dinosaurs and many other kinds of creatures have died out since creation, so, also, many different kinds of horses died out. Evolutionists still search, and will continue to do so, without success, for the transitional forms which must exist, if evolution is true.

Eohippus

WHAT ABOUT DINOSAURS, THOSE TERRIBLE LIZARDS ?

Stories about dinosaurs are fascinating. Is it because of their awesome size or their odd structures, such as big, bony, club-like knobs near the end of their tails, or because some were huge, fierce meat-eaters? Perhaps it is because they are extinct, and we can only imagine what they were like? Most of us have seen fossils of some of the monstrous dinosaurs in natural history museums, and we stand in awe, as we consider what a living creature of such proportions would have been like.

Stegosaurus skeleton

The first fossil of a dinosaur, the *Iguanodon*, was discovered in 1822 by Dr. Gideon Mantell, an English doctor and amateur fossil hunter. At first, Dr. Mantell and the scientists who examined the fossil didn't realize what the creature was. Finally, it was realized that an entirely new kind of creature had been discovered—some of which were extremely large. The famous British anatomist and paleontologist, Sir Richard Owen, who, incidentally, became one of Charles Darwin's strongest opponents, named these creatures "dinosaurs," which means "terrible lizards." The jaws of *Tyrannosaurus rex*, six feet long with teeth six inches long, certainly give credence to the name "terrible lizard."

Dinosaurs in the Bible

Dinosaurs are not mentioned in the Bible, in the sense that the word appears in the Bible, because that name wasn't invented until 1841, and the Bible was translated into English in about 1600—over 200 years earlier—but I do believe that dinosaur are *described* in the Bible! In Job, we read:

*Behold now behemoth, which I made with thee; he eateth grass as an ox. Lo now, his strength is in his loins, and his force is in the navel of his belly. He moveth his tail **like a cedar**: The sinews of his stones are wrapped together. His bones are as strong pieces of brass; his bones are like bars of iron. He is the chief of the ways of God: He that made him can make his sword to approach unto him. Surely the mountains bring him forth food, where all the beasts of the field play. He lieth under the shady trees, in the covert of the reed, and fens. The shady trees cover him with their shadow; the willows of the brook compass him about. Behold, he drinketh up a river, and hasteth not: He trusteth that **he can draw up Jordan into his mouth**. He taketh it with his eyes: His nose pierceth through snares.*

Job 40:15-24

Some have suggested that this passage of Scripture is describing an elephant or perhaps a hippopotamus. However, this creature had a tail like a cedar tree—words which certainly could never be used to describe an elephant or a hippopotamus. Furthermore, the creature described in Job is so huge he could drink up a river and was not in a hurry. One reason he didn't need to hurry was that his massive size insured he need not fear any animal who also would have approached the river to drink.

Dinosaurs, as were all other animals (except for those that lived in the sea and the birds that flew in the air), were created on the sixth day of creation—the same day man was created (note "Behold now behemoth, which **I made with thee . . .**"). Although dinosaurs and man were created to inhabit the earth at the same time, dinosaurs became extinct after the Flood of Noah (which will be explained later in more detail). It wasn't until the fossil remains of these huge creatures began to be discovered in great numbers that modern man acknowledged their true existence.

Dinosaurs — Created or Evolved?

Since the discovery by Dr. Mantell, fossils of dinosaurs have been found on every continent of the world, as far north as Alaska and as far south as Antarctica. Dinosaurs existed in all sizes, shapes, and descriptions. Fossils of dinosaurs provide an ideal test case for creation versus evolution. There were many different *kinds* of dinosaurs. Some were as small as chickens and some were among the largest creatures that ever lived, weighing as much as eighty tons (160,000 pounds). Many of them had very unusual structures. Therefore, if dinosaurs evolved during a period of about 150 million years, beginning with an ordinary kind of reptile (as evolutionists believe), then thousands of intermediate creatures must have existed. During that vast stretch of time, millions of dinosaurs would have lived and died. If evolution is true, our natural history museums should be able to display thousands of indisputable transitional forms. If creation is true, each kind of dinosaur would appear fully formed right from the start, with no intermediate type of fossil to suggest that these dinosaurs had evolved from a common ancestor.

Triceratops

The fossil record of the dinosaur shows clearly that every one of the different *kinds* of dinosaurs appears fully formed, with no evidence that it evolved from an earlier form.

Horned Dinosaurs

There were different kinds of horned dinosaurs. *Triceratops* had three horns—one above each eye and one on the end of the snout. It is estimated he weighed eight to ten tons. He had a huge shield which protected his neck and shoulders and which was composed of bone up to six inches thick. *Triceratops* had both an offensive weapon (the horns) and a defensive weapon (the shield) in the event of attack by other dinosaurs. We do not find a series of transitional forms showing those horns slowly evolving or the armor shield gradually forming.

Stegosaurus, unlike *Triceratops*, had no horns on his small head, and his brain was probably about the size of a walnut. He had four formidable spikes on the end of his tail which were about three feet long and nearly six inches thick at the base. *Stegosaurus* probably used these spikes on the end of his tail much as *Triceratops* used his horns, to ward off attacks by other dinosaurs. *Stegosaurus* also had a series of very unusual plates running down along his neck, body, and tail. Some have suggested that these plates were there for protection, but most

Stegosaurus

likely they were heat exchangers—absorbing heat from the sun on cool days and radiating heat on warm days.

One of the dinosaurs *Triceratops* and *Stegosaurus* would have had to contend with was *Tyrannosaurus*. Both of these dinosaurs would have been able to defend themselves by using their sharp horns or spikes to tear into the soft underbelly of their attacker. The fossil record shows these defensive structures fully formed. There are no fossils of transitional forms showing spikes gradually developing and no fossils of intermediates showing bony plates gradually coming into being on some previously ordinary reptile. No fossil like the above-mentioned has ever been found, nor will it ever be.

Duckbilled Dinosaurs

The duckbilled dinosaur may seem at first to be a very unusual kind of dinosaur. A vast number of duckbilled dinosaurs roamed the earth in ancient times, and numerous fossils of them have been found in many places around the world. These duckbilled dinosaurs include *Corythosaurus, Parasaurolophus, Lambeosaurus,* and *Anatosaurus.* Just recently, a fossil graveyard of duckbilled dinosaurs was found above the Arctic Circle in Alaska. This discovery has evolutionists asking, how could dinosaurs live in an area which is now covered with ice and snow the year round and has six months of darkness each year? This will be discussed at a later time.

Anatosaurus (previously called *Trachodon*) stood about 18 feet high. He had webbed feet and a powerful tail that proved useful in swimming. He had a huge duckbill, with as many as 2,000 teeth piled one on top of each other in the back of his duckbill. These teeth were used to chew the large amount of vegetation needed to maintain this large animal every day. When his teeth got worn and fell out, other teeth were right there ready to take their place.

If, indeed, these many different kinds of duckbilled dinosaurs evolved from reptiles or other kinds of dinosaurs, then the jaws and teeth of reptiles, etc., had to evolve into

Duckbilled dinosaurs: *Corythosaurus, Parasaurolophus, Lambeosaurus,* and *Anatosaurus.*

Anatosaurus skull

duckbills. Since many fossils of duckbilled dinosaurs have been recovered from many parts of the world, and since there are many different kinds of duckbilled dinosaurs (meaning that evolution of duckbilled dinosaurs would have happened many different times), scientists should be able to find thousands of transitional forms showing reptiles or ordinary dinosaurs gradually evolving into duckbilled dinosaurs. Not one such fossil has ever been found! The problem is not with the fossil record! It stands as a silent but undeniable witness to the abrupt appearance of fully formed, massive creatures, created just as described in the Bible.

Meat Eaters

There was also a variety of meat-eating (carnivorous) dinosaurs. Most people assume they ate meat; they appeared to be equipped for it, with huge jaws and teeth that would be efficient for tearing flesh, and with claws and powerful muscles. We have already mentioned *Tyrannosaurus rex*, the biggest meat-eater of all. He is believed to have stood upright approximately 20 feet high, with a total length of 50 feet. Fossilized remains of this creature have been reconstructed with jaws six feet long, containing teeth up to six inches long. It is highly probable that this animal was one of the most feared creatures, by both man and animal alike. It is supposed that his main diet consisted of other dinosaurs, but it also may be that these teeth and claws were used to eat tough roots and bark, etc.

Small Dinosaurs

There was also a variety of small dinosaurs, all of which apparently walked on two feet (bipedal, in contrast to quadrupedal dinosaurs, or those that walked on four feet). These included *Podokesaurus*, *Compsognathus*, and *Struthiomimus*. These small dinosaurs may have fed on a variety of plants, and may have eaten small reptiles, mammals, and eggs. *Struthiomimus* means "ostrich mimic," and he was so named because it is believed that he looked like an ostrich. *Struthiomimus* may have looked like an ostrich, but he never could have been an ancestor of the ostrich. First of all, *Struthiomimus* didn't have even a hint of a feather. Secondly, he didn't have the right kind of hips. Dinosaurs had

Struthiomimus

two different kinds of hips. "Lizard-hipped" dinosaurs obviously had hips similar to lizards and other reptiles, while the "bird-hipped" dinosaurs had hips similar to birds. *Struthiomimus*, as did all others of these small bipedal dinosaurs, had "lizard hips." Thus, it did not have the right kind of hips to be the ancestor of birds. Thirdly, not a single transitional form between *Struthiomimus* and an ostrich or any other bird has ever been found.

Big Plant Eaters

Diplodocus ("double-beamed") had a very long neck and tail, with a total length of approximately 100 feet. *Brontosaurus* ("thunder lizard") was so named because the ground must have thundered when he walked by. *Brontosaurus* (recently re-identified by dinosaur specialists as *Apatosaurus*) was about 80 feet long and weighed about 40 tons. He also was a plant-eater. He was not the biggest dinosaur of all, however. Recently a fossil of a *Brachiosaurus* has been found which, to date, is the largest dinosaur on record. He may have stood 50 feet high (as high as a five-story building) and may have weighed as much as 80 tons—twice as large as *Brontosaurus*. He had a unique location for his nostrils: in a bony dome on the top of his head!

It has been surmised that perhaps the location of his nostrils enabled him to dash out into a lake or stream to escape a hungry meat-eating dinosaur and then raise his head out of the water just enough to breathe. We cannot know the many reasons why God designed the *Brachiosaurus* as He did, but one thing we do know for certain: No one has ever found a single transitional form showing the nostrils migrating from the snout up into the bony dome on the top of the head. When he first appears in the fossil record, *Brachiosaurus* is 100 percent *Brachiosaurus*, nostrils and all.

Fossil graveyard

That is true of every dinosaur ever found, whether *Brachiosaurus, Brontosaurus, Tyrannosaurus, Struthiomimus, Stegosaurus, Triceratops,* or any other dinosaur. Dinosaurs were some of the "beasts of the earth" mentioned in Genesis 1:24,25, created on the sixth day. Dinosaur fossils give eloquent testimony to the fact of creation.

What Happened to the Dinosaurs?

Why did dinosaurs die out, along with flying reptiles, marine reptiles, and many other creatures that used to populate the earth? How could they be so numerous, and thus so successful and in such variety—meat-eaters, plant-eaters, little, big, ordinary, bizarre, slow, fast—and yet become utterly extinct? Scientists have puzzled over this question since dinosaur fossils were discovered, and many ideas have been suggested. Perhaps a peculiar disease wiped them out. Some evolutionists speculate the newly evolved mammals ate all the dinosaur eggs. One of the latest ideas is that an asteroid struck the earth and threw billions of tons of dust and debris into the air. The dust was so thick it blacked out the sun for several years and caused most of the plants on the earth to die. Therefore, most of the plant-eating dinosaurs died, and left little for the meat-eating dinosaurs to eat.

There are things wrong with all of these assumptions. For example, if an asteroid collision caused the dinosaurs to die, why didn't alligators, turtles, snakes, and all other reptiles die? If tough dinosaurs died out (large and small), why didn't thin-skinned mammals become extinct? How could a great variety of birds survive? Scientists, by and large, simply do not know why dinosaurs died out.

I believe that by combining the facts of science with the facts we find in the Bible, we can make a reasonable assumption. The Bible tells us, in Genesis Chapters 6-8, about a great Flood—the Flood of Noah—that overflowed the entire earth and destroyed every land-dwelling, air-breathing creature on the earth except those on the Ark. The Bible tells us that it rained for 40 days and 40 nights. This could not happen today. If one or two inches of rain would fall over the entire surface

"And every living substance was destroyed which was upon the face of the ground, both man, and cattle, and the creeping things, and the fowl of the heaven; and they were destroyed from the earth: and Noah only remained alive, and they that were with him in the ark."Genesis 7:23

of the earth, the atmosphere would be bone dry. There is just not enough water vapor in the atmosphere today to keep it raining for 40 days and nights over the entire earth.

That tells us that there had to be much more water vapor in the atmosphere before the Flood than there is today. Most of that water vapor came down as rain at the time of the Flood, and, because of drastically changed conditions, only a small fraction of the quantity of the pre-Flood water vapor was able to return to the atmosphere. The amount of water vapor in the atmosphere today is much, much less than existed before the Flood.

There are three gases in our atmosphere today that are responsible for the absorption and retention of heat from the sun. These gases are ozone, carbon dioxide, and water vapor. Of these, water vapor is the most important. If there were much more water vapor in the atmosphere before the Flood than there is today, that water vapor would have absorbed and held in much more heat from the sun than the atmosphere does today. This would create what is called a "greenhouse" effect, and would cause a worldwide mild, warm climate. Lush vegetation would cover the earth. It would be mildly warm, even at the North and South Poles.

The atmosphere lost most of its water vapor at the time of the Flood. This caused a drastic change in the climate on the earth. The worldwide, uniform mild climate of pre-Flood days was replaced by present conditions, with climatic zones that include the frigid Arctic and Antarctic zones, a temperate zone, and a tropical zone. Vast deserts now cover areas which once were covered with lush vegetation and forests. Thus, when the dinosaurs and all other creatures emerged from the Ark, they came out into a world that was drastically different from that in which they had flourished before. Many of these creatures, including the dinosaurs, failed to survive in the new world. How long did it take them to die out? A year? Ten years? Fifty years? Longer? We don't know, but it is certain that they did, indeed, die out. When these few creatures died, no fossils were formed. The fossils of dinosaurs that we find today were likely formed at the time of the Flood.

Much geological evidence exists that the earth had a worldwide mild climate at one time. Fossils of palm trees and ferns are found on Greenland, so although it is now covered all year with ice and snow, at one time Greenland had a climate similar to the Caribbean. The fossil graveyard of duck-billed

Fossil fern

dinosaurs, found recently on the north shore of Alaska, is evidence that this part of the world enjoyed a much milder climate when it was home to these animals. Other fossils of animals that now live only in the tropics have been found above the Arctic Circle.

Evolutionary geologists do not know what could have caused these tremendous changes in the climate of the earth. This is because they cannot believe what the Bible says about the Flood. If they do, they would have to believe what it says about creation.

Dinosaurs on the Ark?

The Ark was 450 feet long, 45 feet tall, 75 feet wide by 3 decks = 100,000 square feet of floor space.

Did all the animals fit on the Ark, including the dinosaurs? How could Noah put millions of species of animals on the Ark? Where would he put a 50-foot high, 80-ton *Brachiosaurus*? It was not necessary to put huge, adult dinosaurs on the Ark. The preservation of the kinds was served just as well by preserving baby dinosaurs. This would greatly simplify the size issue. Furthermore, millions of species were not put on the Ark. The Bible tells us that God said two of each "kind" of *land-dwelling, air-breathing* creatures were to be placed on the Ark, except for the "clean" animals suitable for sacrifice—seven of each of these were placed there. Today, there are about 20,000 species of land-dwelling, air-breathing creatures in existence (i.e., mammals, birds, reptiles, amphibians). If we assume that another 20,000 species have become extinct, then 40,000 species, or approximately 80,000 animals had to fit on the Ark.

Some of those animals are big, but many of them, like rats, mice, lizards, and birds, are quite small. The average size of all these animals would be approximately equivalent to the size of sheep. The Ark was about 450 feet long, 45 feet high, and 75 feet wide. That means that, with its three decks, the Ark had slightly more than 100,000 square feet of floor space. These 80,000 animals could be caged in an area of approximately 50,000 square feet, leaving half the Ark's space for storage of food, air space, living space for Noah and his family, etc. Furthermore, it is possible God caused most of the animals to hibernate, in order to minimize the problems involved in their care. The Flood was an event brought upon the earth by God, and it was His will that Noah, his family, and two of every land-dwelling, air-breathing creature should survive, including the "terrible lizards!"

75

Chapter 7

DID WE COME FROM ADAM OR FROM THE APES?

Creation of Man and Woman

And God said, Let Us make man in Our image, after Our likeness: And let them have dominion over the fish of the sea, and over the fowl of the air, and over the cattle, and over all the earth, and over every creeping thing that creepeth upon the earth.

So God created man in His own image, in the image of God created He him; male and female created He them.

Genesis 1:26,27

And the Lord God formed man of the dust of the ground, and breathed into his nostrils the breath of life; and man became a living soul.

And the Lord God caused a deep sleep to fall upon Adam, and he slept: And He took one of his ribs, and closed up the flesh instead thereof;

And the rib, which the Lord God had taken from man, made He a woman, and brought her unto the man.

Genesis 2:7,21,22

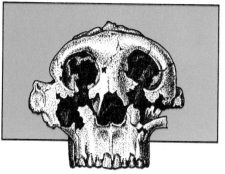

Three different interpretations of what the fossil *Australopithecus boisei* looked like from the same skull remains. This shows the imagination of scientists and artists. Such "reconstructions" can be made ape-like or human, depending on the artist's viewpoint or belief system.

Did God create man in the image of an ape? No, He created man in the image of God. Thus, from what the Bible says, we know that evolution cannot possibly be correct. People did not evolve from apes. God first created man by taking the elements found in the dust of the ground and forming Adam. We note that Adam did not become a living person until God breathed into his nostrils the breath of life. Then God made the first woman, Eve, in a very special way, by removing one of Adam's ribs, from which He created Eve.

Why did God create woman in this way? The Bible doesn't tell us, but perhaps God did it that way to impress upon mankind the closeness and dependence of the wife upon her husband, and of the husband upon his wife. In the New Testament, we find further proof of this special way that God created woman. In I Corinthians 11:8, we read, "For the man is not of the woman; but the woman of the man." Today, of course, we are all born from a woman—we all have mothers. Thus, in his letter to the Corinthians, the Apostle Paul was referring to that special moment in history when God created man and woman. The first man was not born of a woman, but Adam was first specially created, and then Eve was created from Adam. Evolutionists, of course, do not believe that God created people. They do not believe that Adam and Eve ever really existed. They believe that humans evolved from ape-like creatures, beginning millions of years ago. Thus, it is impossible to believe in evolution and also to believe what the Bible tells us about creation.

Ape-Men?

What about cavemen? Weren't the Neanderthals a primitive people who were not quite human? What about "Lucy" and her fellow creatures? Were they ancestors of man? Were they little ape-like creatures who walked upright in a human manner? Pictures in schoolbooks, in magazines, in newspapers, and on television, show creatures who supposedly lived millions of years ago and who were partway between apes and people. If these creatures did indeed exist, this would be powerful evidence for evolution. However, evolutionists' faith in their theory makes it necessary for them to believe that a tooth, or a piece of a skull, or a jawbone, or some other fossil bone came from a creature partway between ape and man. When all of the evidence is carefully and thoroughly studied by the best scientific methods, however, it turns out that these

78

fossils were either from monkeys, apes, or people, and not from something that was part ape and part human.

When a person believes in something very strongly, he often "sees" evidence that supports his belief, even though it doesn't really exist, and he pays little attention to things that contradict what he believes. Scientists are human, thus they are subject to human error. Evolutionists believe that people have evolved from apes, so they expect to find evidence to support that theory. Oftentimes they are certain they have found evidence that a fossil is from a creature partway between an ape and a human, but they are badly mistaken. What they thought they were seeing really did not exist at all. Let us look at some examples:

The Piltdown Hoax

In 1912, Charles Dawson, a lawyer and amateur fossil hunter, discovered a few fragments of a jawbone and pieces of a skull in a gravel pit near Piltdown, England. The jawbone appeared to be quite ape-like, but the teeth and the skull appeared to be quite human-like. Dawson and the English scientists with whom he consulted were certain that all of these fossil bones were from a single individual—a creature combining human-like and ape-like features. It is amazing how many supposed human-like characteristics they thought they could see in the ape-like jaw and how many ape-like characteristics they imagined they were seeing in the human skull. They declared that these fossils were from a creature intermediate between ape and man that existed 500,000 years ago. This creature was given the official name of *Eoanthropus dawsoni* (*Eoanthropus* means "Dawn-man") and he became known as the famous Piltdown Man. Although some scientists did not believe that all these bones came from the same individual, most scientists declared that Piltdown Man was a genuine subhuman ancestor of man. For nearly 50 years, Piltdown Man stood as one of our ancestors, and about *500* books and pamphlets were written about Piltdown Man.

But in 1950, Piltdown Man got "buried" again! In that year, it was shown that Piltdown Man was a hoax—a fake! Someone had taken the jawbone of an ape and the skull of a modern human, treated them with chemicals to make them *look* old, filed the teeth with a file to make them look human-like instead of ape-like, planted the "fossil" bones in the gravel pit, and fooled the world's greatest experts! Why did it take the experts

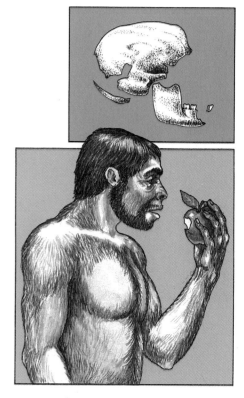

Piltdown Man—proven in 1950 to be a hoax.

almost 50 years to detect the fraud? Why didn't they see the scratch marks on the teeth made by the file when they first looked at the teeth? Why didn't they notice, right away, that the brown stain on these bones was only in a thin, outer layer? Why were they able to "see" human characteristics in the ape's jaw, and why did they "see" ape-like characteristics in the human skull? All of this happened because evolutionists believed so strongly in evolution that they *saw the things* they expected to find, and *failed to see* things they did not want to see.

Nebraska Man

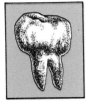

In 1922, a *single tooth* was discovered in western Nebraska. The tooth was shown to one of America's foremost fossil experts, Dr. Henry Fairfield Osborn, professor at Columbia University. Dr. Osborn and other American experts were very excited by the appearance of this tooth. They declared that they could see, in that tooth, certain characteristics intermediate between ape and man. In fact, they weren't quite sure whether it was from an ape-like man or a man-like ape. He was given the official name of *Hesperopithecus*, became popularly known as Nebraska Man, and was presented as *evidence* that man had evolved from apes. In 1922, the *Illustrated London News* published a picture of Nebraska Man, his wife, and the tools they were using—all based upon the discovery of one single tooth!

Nebraska Man—created from the discovery of a single tooth.

A few years after the discovery of the tooth, some additional bones of the creature were discovered and Nebraska Man turned out to be neither an ape-like man nor a man-like ape. He turned out to be a *pig*! That's right—Nebraska Man was nothing more than a pig's tooth!

Neanderthal Man

In 1860, about the time that Darwin published his book on evolution, the first few fossil fragments of Neanderthal Man were found in the Neanderthal Valley, in Germany. Later, additional fossils of the Neanderthal people were found in other parts of Europe, in Asia, Africa, and Israel. In 1908, a nearly complete skeleton was found in France. The Neanderthal people manufactured tools and weapons, and they buried their dead just like modern-day people. Furthermore, their brains were somewhat larger than those of modern-day humans. All of this indicated that they were fully human, *Homo sapiens*. They did, in some ways, however, appear to be rather primitive. Their skulls were flatter than ours, some of them had rather heavy eyebrow ridges, and the skeleton in France appeared to be hunched over, as if Neanderthal Man did not walk completely upright like you and I. Based on these findings, the Neanderthal people were declared, by evolutionists, to be subhuman ancestors of man, and were given the official name of *Homo neanderthalensis*. Museum exhibits and pictures of the Neanderthal people portrayed them as sort of long-armed, knuckle-dragging, beetle-browed, stooped-shouldered, bow-legged subhumans.

A famous anatomist, Dr. Rudolph Virchow, declared, many years ago, that the primitive features of the Neanderthal people were not due to the fact that these people were subhuman, but were due to diseases, or pathological conditions. He pointed out that the skeleton discovered in France was of an old man who couldn't walk upright because he had a bad case of arthritis! Dr. Virchow declared, further, that all of these people suffered severely from rickets (a condition caused by the lack of Vitamin D) which causes bones to become soft and deformed. For many years, however, evolutionists paid no attention to what Dr. Virchow was saying, because they wanted Neanderthal Man to be a true subhuman ancestor of man.

Eventually, however, other skeletons of Neanderthal people were found that were fully erect, and it was established, by medical research, that the skeleton found in France was, indeed, that of an arthritic old man. X-rays of the fossil bones and teeth showed, just as Dr. Virchow had declared, that all of the Neanderthal people had rickets. Scientists finally concluded that all of the so-called primitive features of the Neanderthal people were due to pathological conditions, or diseases. Museums have removed the old exhibits of Neanderthal people and have replaced them with new exhibits showing the Neanderthal people looking very human, and about 30 years ago, two scientists published an article about Neanderthal people in which they declared that if Neanderthal Man were given a shave, a haircut, and a bath, put into a business suit, and placed on the New York subway, no one would take a second look!

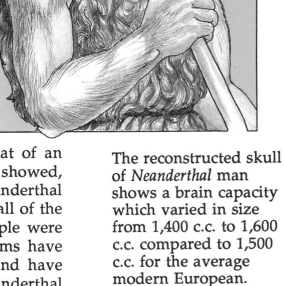

The reconstructed skull of *Neanderthal* man shows a brain capacity which varied in size from 1,400 c.c. to 1,600 c.c. compared to 1,500 c.c. for the average modern European.

81

From a few isolated teeth and upper and lower jaw fragments, a complete creature called *Ramapithacus* was imagined.

Australopithecus robustus—
reconstructed head to toe on the basis of several craniums, more than a dozen jaws, and hundreds of teeth from two south African caves.

Ramapithecus

About 60 years ago, part of a fossilized jaw and a few teeth were discovered in India, of a creature given the name *Ramapithecus*. Some famous experts declared, however, that these fossils proved this creature was on its way to becoming man, and that he walked upright, like humans. In the past few years, however, enough of this creature has been found to show that he was an orangutan. The experts now admit that *Ramapithecus* was not an ancestor of man at all.

Orce Man

Just recently, a skull cap was found in Spain, and was declared by Spanish experts to be the skull cap of the oldest fossil man ever discovered in Europe. He was named Orce Man, for the village near where he was found. However, French experts were able to confirm that the skull cap was that of a six-month-old donkey!

Piltdown Man was not our ancestor! He was a hoax constructed from the jawbone of an ape and a human skull. Nebraska Man was not our ancestor! He was fabricated from a pig's tooth. Neanderthal Man was our ancestor! He was 100 percent man. *Ramapithecus* and Orce Man were not our ancestors! One was an orangutan, and one a donkey! The supposed evolutionary family tree of man is barren of the fossil evidence necessary to give credence to their theories.

Australopithecus

What about the other suggested ancestors for man? There is not adequate space to discuss all of the current candidates that evolutionists are suggesting as our ancestors, but we will discuss one of the most often cited—*Australopithecus* (pronounced aw-stra-lo-pi-the-kuss). For many years now, *Australopithecus* has been the key figure in most human evolutionary schemes.

If humans did evolve from apes millions of years ago, there would have been hundreds, perhaps thousands of species, intermediate, or transitional, between man and the apes. It is strange then, that after more than 100 years of searching for the fossils of these species, evolutionists have been able to find only two or three, and these are highly questionable.

In 1924, Dr. Raymond Dart discovered the first fossil of *Australopithecus* in South Africa. The name *Australopithecus* means "southern ape" (australo = southern; pithecus = ape). It was the skull of a creature believed to be very young—possibly six years old or less. It was very ape-like, but Dr. Dart believed that the teeth were more human-like than those found in modern apes, so he declared that this creature was on its way to becoming human. Many of his fellow evolutionists disagreed with him at that time, and maintained that *Australopithecus* was nothing more than an ape. As time went by, however, more and more evolutionists adopted Dart's theory. Other fossils of these creatures were found throughout South Africa. Then, in 1959, Dr. Louis Leakey and his wife, Mary, discovered a fossil skull in Tanzania, in East Africa. Dr. Leakey named his creature *Zinjanthropus* (East Africa Man). He declared that no one had ever found such a creature before, and that it was an intermediate between ape and man. Overnight, Dr. Leakey became famous for his discovery, but later on Dr. Leakey and other anthropologists agreed that *Zinjanthropus* was also a variety, or species, of *Australopithecus*. Although all of these creatures were very ape-like, most evolutionists theorized they walked upright in a near-human manner.

Lucy

In 1973, Dr. Donald Johanson, an American anthropologist, discovered fossils of creatures in Ethiopia, to which he gave the name *Australopithecus afarensis*. One of the creatures was a female, with about 40 percent of the fossilized skeleton intact. Johanson gave her the name "Lucy." Although Johanson admits that, from the neck up, "Lucy" was ape (she had the jaws, teeth, face, and brain of an ape), he still maintained she walked upright just like a human. Johnson quickly became famous, and everyone in the world who has subsequently studied anthropology knows about "Lucy," because, according to Johanson, "Lucy" was an ape that walked erect, thus was on its way to becoming human.

Today, most evolutionists believe that "Lucy" and all other *Australopithecines* walked upright, and were in the line that led to man.

Lucy—when they required a knee joint to prove that Lucy walked upright, they used one found more than 200 feet lower in the strata and more than two miles away.

83

Man Did Not Evolve

Lord Zuckerman (Dr. Solly Zuckerman), a famous British anatomist, was for many years the head of the Department of Anatomy at the medical school of the University of Birmingham, in England. He was first knighted for his distinguished scientific career (becoming Sir Solly Zuckerman), and later became Lord Zuckerman. He had a team of scientists, rarely numbering less than four, who studied the fossils of *Australopithecus* for 15 years. They used the most sophisticated methods of anatomical study available to analyze these fossils. After many years of study and research, Lord Zuckerman declared that *Australopithecus* did *not* walk upright, and that these creatures were *not* intermediate between ape and man. Lord Zuckerman's team concluded that they were not the same as any modern ape living today, but they were, nevertheless, nothing more than apes. His final conclusions are found in a book he published in 1970, *Beyond the Ivory Tower*. In that book, he has two chapters about his research on the origin of man. On page 64 of this book, Lord Zuckerman makes a very important admission. He says that if we exclude the possibility of creation, then, obviously, man must have evolved from an ape-like creature; but if he did, there is no evidence for it in the fossil record. Lord Zuckerman makes no profession of being a creationist. If the evidence supported evolution, he would readily accept it. He must admit, however, that there is simply no evidence in the fossil record to support the notion that man has evolved.

Chimps and mankind remain distinct and separate and the fossil record continues to widen the gulf between man and ape.

Dr. Charles Oxnard, one of Lord Zuckerman's former students, is now Professor of Anatomy and Director of Graduate Studies at the University of Southern California Medical School. For many years, he has studied the postcranial skeleton (that portion of the skeleton below the skull) of *Australopithecus*. He employed the very latest techniques for his research. Dr. Oxnard, even though he is not a creationist, has declared that his research has established that these creatures *did not* walk upright like humans, that they *were not* intermediate between apes and man, and that, certainly, they *were not the ancestors of man.*

Other scientists have come to somewhat similar conclusions. As more and more fossils are found and more evidence becomes available, I am certain that "Lucy" and her fellow *Australopithecus* creatures are going to be dismissed from the family tree of man by evolutionists, themselves. Right now, *Australopithecus* is one of the most important branches on the evolutionary family tree of man. When that branch is cut off and discarded, there won't be much of the tree left.

Evolutionists still maintain that humans and modern apes evolved from a common ancestor that existed millions of years ago. That hypothetical common ancestor is just a phantom creature, however, for no one has ever been able to find any trace of him. *Ramapithecus* was once believed to have been one of the earliest branches leading to man, but as we described earlier, he turned out to be an orangutan. With the similar casting out of Piltdown Man, Nebraska Man, and Neanderthal Man as branches on the family tree, and now *Australopithecus*, the tree has become very bare, indeed. In fact, only *Homo erectus* (Java Man and Peking Man) will be left as serious contenders.

However, in my book, *Evolution: The Challenge of the Fossil Record* (Master Books, El Cajon, California), I describe in detail why I believe that Java Man and Peking Man were not the ancestors of man, but were apes. In fact, Dr. Eugene Dubois, the discoverer of Java Man and the one who first claimed that Java Man was an ancestor of man, changed his mind about 15 years before he died, and declared that Java Man was nothing more than a giant ape—more particularly, a giant gibbon. On the other hand, everyone now agrees that the once loudly proclaimed Cro-Magnon Man was identical to a modern European.

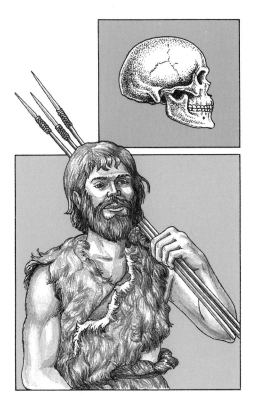

Cro-Magnon

Apes From Man?

R ecently, an astounding development has taken place. In the last few years, several evolutionists have declared they now believe that rather than man evolving from apes, apes evolved from humans! Even though all the evolutionists in the world are looking at exactly the same evidence, some are now saying that apes evolved from man. This theory is exactly opposite of the evolutionary idea that man evolved from apes. The reason two such contradictory theories can be arrived at from the same set of evidence, is that these scientists begin with a basic assumption that is wrong—that is, that evolution has taken place. If fossil evidence is viewed in the light of creation, such contradictions and problems vanish.

The Bible very clearly states, in unmistakable language, that God created man and woman in a very special way. The facts of science, as found in the fossil record, provide powerful positive evidence to support the Biblical record of creation.

Embryology

Many science books teach that the facts of embryology support evolution—that the human embryo has gill slits just like fish, and this proves that hundreds of millions of years ago, we had a fish as our distant ancestor. This theory is called the theory of *embryological recapitulation*. According to this idea, as the human embryo (or any other embryo) develops, it recapitulates its evolutionary ancestry. That is, it resembles each evolutionary ancestor in the correct order of evolution. Thus, the human embryo starts out as a single cell. Later, it supposedly looks like a fish (with gill slits), then it looks like a tadpole (the larval stage of an amphibian). Then, later, it resembles a reptile, then an ape, and, finally, becomes human. This theory was very popular during Darwin's time. In fact, Darwin declared that the best evidence for evolution came from the study of embryology.

Today, the theory of embryological recapitulation is no longer believed by most evolutionists, and certainly not by embryologists, even though it is still found in many textbooks. During a debate a few years ago, Dr. Ashley Montagu, at Princeton University, one of the world's foremost evolutionists admitted that the theory of embryological recapitulation had been proven to be wrong, and that no evolutionist should ever use this discredited theory to support evolution.

The human embryo has no gill slits. It does have a series of bars and grooves in the neck region which resemble structures in the neck region of a fish embryo, which do develop into gills. In the human embryo, however, none of these structures ever open into the throat to become slits, and none ever develop into gills.

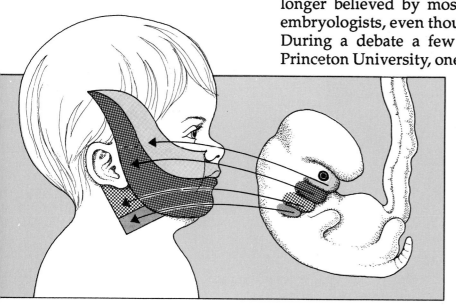

The so-called gill slits in the embryo are in reality pharyngeal pouches that develop into the lower jaw, parts of the middle ear and certain glands.

Furthermore, in the human embryo, the tongue develops before the teeth, the heart before the blood vessels, and the brain before the nerve cords. This is the opposite order that would be expected if the embryo were repeating the supposed evolutionary process. Just recently, an instrument has been developed called a fetoscope, which can be inserted into the mother's uterus to observe and photograph the embryo as it develops. Using this instrument, scientists discovered that at every stage of its development, the human embryo is totally human. God has programmed the embryo of each creature to start out as a single cell, and to develop into a new-born creature completely prepared to survive and thrive in the world into which it is born.

Before I formed thee in the belly I knew thee; and before thou camest forth out of the womb I sanctified thee, and I ordained thee a prophet unto the nations.

Jeremiah 1:5

Vestigial Organs

Evolutionists have also claimed that within our bodies are structures and organs which now have no function, but which were useful to our evolutionary ancestors. These organs and structures are called *vestigial organs*, the idea being that now they are only useless vestiges of once-useful structures. Approximately 100 years ago, a German scientist named Wiedersheim listed 180 structures and organs in man which he thought were now useless. He included, for example, the pituitary gland, the thymus gland, the pineal gland, the tonsils, the appendix, and the coccyx, or tailbone. After a century of scientific and medical research, we now know that all of these structures have an important function in man, and, in fact, without many of them, we cannot live. The pituitary, thymus, and pineal glands are vital to our existence. The tonsils and the appendix are now known to be, among other things, important disease-fighting organs. The tailbone serves to anchor certain pelvic muscles. You cannot sit comfortably without it, and it protects the end of the spinal column. In a scientific journal, not long ago, an evolutionist published an article in which he declared that supposed vestigial organs offer no support for evolution.

Homology

Another evidence used by evolutionists to support evolution is the fact that there are many similar structures in different animals. Thus, the forelimbs, or arms, of humans are similar to the forelimbs of apes, monkeys, most other mammals, birds, reptiles, and amphibians. The human eye is very similar to the eyes found in all other mammals, reptiles, birds, amphibians, and fish. We all have what is called the vertebrate eye. The evolutionist says these similar (homologous) structures in different animals exist because we have evolved from common ancestors. Thus, all mammals (as well as man), reptiles, birds, amphibians, and fish, have the same kind of eyes because they must have evolved from a common ancestor. The creationist maintains that similar structures exist in different animals because God, the Master Engineer, created similar structures for similar needs. We see this in human engineering. All bridges are not identical, but engineers, utilizing their knowledge and training, build all bridges according to good engineering principles. Thus, most bridges are quite similar.

Sir Gavin de Beer was a British biologist and evolutionist. He did careful research on the subject of homology. To his surprise and dismay, he discovered that the scientific evidence related to homologous organs and structures was very much against what he would expect as an evolutionist. The evidence did not fit evolutionary theory. He declared that evolutionists were wrong when they claimed that homologous structures exist because they had been inherited from a common ancestor, and published a book entitled *Homology, An Unsolved Problem* (Oxford Biology Reader #11, Oxford University Press, 1971). To evolutionists, similar structures are still an unsolved problem, but this fact is no mystery to creationists. God created those similar structures in different animals as a means of augmenting similar functions.

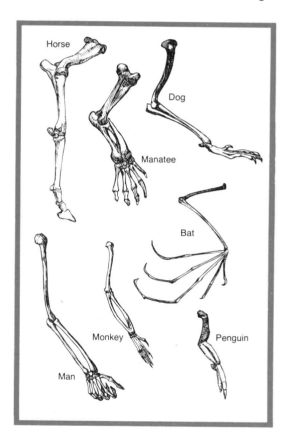

Homology—the study of similar structures in different animals.

88

In the preceding paragraphs, it has been shown that man could not have evolved from apes, and that the evidence

supports the Biblical record of creation. Many questions have been raised about the Biblical history of man, such as, "where did Cain and Abel get their wives?" and "how did all the different human races come into existence if we all came from Adam and Eve?" Cain and Abel married their sisters. This was not wrong in the very beginning of the human race, for two reasons: First, God did not create many couples, He created one, Adam and Eve, so it was necessary for their children to marry among themselves. The second reason is that in the beginning, there were no health problems caused by intermarriage. Adam and Eve were created perfect. They had no bad genes to pass on to their children, such as the genes that cause sickle-cell anemia, diabetes, blindness, sterility, and many other crippling conditions.

"The human eye is very similar to the eyes found in all other mammals, reptiles, birds, amphibians and fish."

As we have described earlier, in Chapter 4, each person has 46 chromosomes. We receive 23 chromosomes from each parent. Thus, all genes occur in pairs. For example, the offspring receives one gene from each parent for eye color. There is a variety of genes for different eye colors. If a gene for brown eyes is inherited from each parent, of course the child will be brown-eyed. If a gene for brown eyes is received from one parent and a gene for blue eyes from the other parent, the child will be brown-eyed, because the gene for brown eyes is *dominant*, and the gene for blue eyes is *recessive*. Such a person, even though he has brown eyes, is said to be a *carrier* for blue eyes, since he has genes for both brown and blue eyes. Since the gene for blue eyes is recessive, one must inherit a

All bridges serve the same basic function but utilize different engineering principles.

gene for blue eyes from both parents in order for the offspring to have blue eyes.

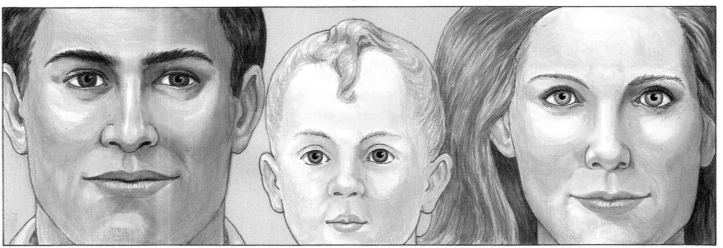

Because brown genes are dominant, a brown-eyed parent and a blue- eyed parent usually have a brown-eyed baby.

Most of the genes that cause genetic diseases, such as sickle-cell anemia, are also recessive. Thus, if one of these "bad" genes is inherited from one parent, but the same gene that is normal is inherited from the other parent, the normal gene is dominant, and the child will be healthy. If one or more bad gene exists within a family, and if a sister would marry a brother, or an uncle a niece, or if first cousins marry, there is a likely possibility that each parent, even though healthy, will be carrying the bad gene, and the child will be a victim of the genetic disease. This is why inter-marriage within today's families is not only strongly discouraged, but is, in fact, unlawful, in most countries of the world.

Of course, this situation did not exist in the family of Adam and Eve. When God created them, all of their genes were perfect. After Adam and Eve sinned, the whole world came under God's curse, bringing about death, disease, pain, and suffering. Scientists are uncertain as to exactly how the curse affected the genetic structure of living things, but they do know that bad genes are caused by mutations. Mutations occur when a good gene is changed slightly, due to the effect of x-rays, cosmic rays, ultraviolet light, chemicals, etc. Mutations began to occur after the curse, but because of the strength of the genetic code created by God, it was many generations after Adam and Eve before bad genes became a problem. Although Cain, Abel, and Seth are the only children of Adam and Eve mentioned by name in the Bible, Genesis 5:4 tells us they had "sons and daughters." Taking into consideration the longevity of man in the pre-Flood world, there would have been an ample population, even among Adam and Eve's own children, from which to choose a spouse.

Origin of Races

About ten years ago, a prominent evolutionist mentioned that it was rather astounding that more than 100 years after Darwin, evolutionists still had no explanation for the origin of human races. Yes, that is astounding! Evolutionists try to explain the greatest mysteries of all—the origin of the universe, the origin of life, the origin of plants and animals, and the origin of man, but, they are baffled by what should be, by comparison, the easiest to explain—the origin of human races. In explaining the origin of "races," one doesn't have to explain something that existed supposedly millions of years ago, in the distant, unobservable past. All of the genetic evidence is available right now, in *living human beings*. If evolution is true, it ought to be a rather simple matter to put the pieces of the genetic jigsaw puzzle together, using evolutionary theory. The problem is, the pieces don't go together, according to evolutionary theory.

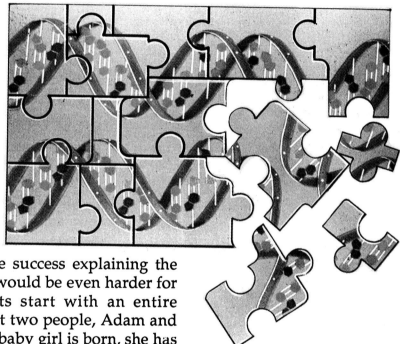

Genetic jigsaw puzzle

Since evolutionists have had little success explaining the origin of races, it would seem that it would be even harder for creationists. After all, evolutionists start with an entire population; creationists start with just two people, Adam and Eve. However, consider this: When a baby girl is born, she has 500,000 eggs in her ovaries. She could potentially produce 500,000 different children, none of whom would be identical. Of course, she will, in all probability, have only a few children. Each male is also born with a great genetic potential. Adam and Eve were each created with the ability to produce a large number of children, none of whom (unless twins, of course) would be identical.

Adam and Eve were not white, black, Oriental, or of any other particular race. They, no doubt, were what we understand today as racially mixed. Their children were all likewise a mixture of the genetic traits that have subsequently produced the races. Among these offspring, one would be able to see tendencies toward various races, but since all marriages were

91

mixed, no races emerged. Even after the Flood (Genesis 6-8), all humans on the earth were the descendants of the three sons and three daughters-in-law of Noah and his wife, and so they, too, must have been racially mixed. As they and their descendants repopulated the earth, all peoples intermarried freely, and there was no isolation of genetic characteristics that would produce features inherent in one particular race. At the Tower of Babel, however, God split the human population into small groups, by "confounding" the one language they spoke into many different languages. Each group of people spoke only the language that God gave them. They could no longer talk to the people in the other groups, so, of course, they no longer intermarried with them. Soon the various groups began to migrate to other parts of the world, and became geographically isolated from one another. Thus, there was necessarily a lot of intermarriage within each group. That is, it was necessary to find marriage partners from the few people within one's own group, and the children of such marriages also had limited choices. When there are marriages of this kind, a concentration of certain genes is developed. If, for example, the group had a concentration of genes for dark skin and negroid features, then a negro people would result. If the group had a concentration of genes found in Oriental people, then the group would give rise to one of the Oriental races. If, on the other hand, the group had a concentration of genes for fair skin and blue eyes, one of the Scandinavian races would emerge.

"Therefore is the name of it called Babel; because the Lord did there confound the language of all the earth: and from thence did the Lord scatter them abroad upon the face of all the earth." *Genesis* 11:9

Evolutionists, themselves, admit that in order for "races"—or sub-species—to arise, a population must be split into small, isolated groups, leading to "inbreeding." What better way to do this than what occurred at the Tower of Babel, as described in Genesis, Chapter 11? To evolutionists, the origin of races still remains an unsolved problem. Creationists, however, utilizing modern genetic studies and the facts of history recorded in the Bible, do have the true explanation for the origin of races. There are no contradictions between the facts of science and the truth recorded in the Word of God, though there are contradictions between the theory of evolution and the Bible. Furthermore, utilizing many facts revealed in the Bible helps us to solve some important scientific problems.

Actually, the concept of "race" is, itself, an evolutionary idea, not a Biblical one. Neither the word nor the idea of "races" is found in the Bible. Today, many evolutionists are also abandoning the concept of "race," realizing there is really only one race—the *human* race!

Cavemen

One of the many questions that keep people from believing the Bible is true, is "who were the cavemen?"—people like the Neanderthal people. Where did they come from? Creationists believe that the Neanderthal people, the Cro-Magnon people, and other so-called cavemen were the descendents of Noah and his family. After the Tower of Babel, the human population split into small groups and migrated into different parts of the world. After this separation, the people in those groups that moved a considerable distance away from other groups, no longer had contact with other people. Once they became isolated in small groups, perhaps they no longer learned by exchanging ideas with other groups. Perhaps they were able to obtain enough food by hunting and gathering, and so gave up agriculture, and when they needed shelter during the cold

winter time, they would live in caves. They thus became "cavemen." Even today, in parts of Africa, South America, and the South Pacific, there are people who live like these "cavemen," living by hunting and gathering, and using bows and arrows, spears, and tools of stone and bone.

Chapter

TESTIMONIES TO GOD'S MARVELOUS CREATION

Bishop Paley and the Watchmaker

Nearly 200 years ago, a British clergyman, Bishop William Paley, wrote a book about the evidences for the existence of God. He argued that there were many examples of living creatures that were incredibly complex, and which exhibited design and purpose. He maintained that these creatures had to be created by an intelligent Creator. In doing so, he employed what became known as the Watchmaker argument. He pointed out that a watch exhibits purposefulness—it tells time. He then described how complex a watch is. Only a trained watchmaker knows how to put it together. He pointed out that everything about the structure and function of the watch demonstrates purposefulness. He then described the way the watch was organized according to an intelligent master plan, so that each part performs its function and the watch operates to accomplish its purpose. He argued that this complex organization had to have an organizer, the grand master plan had to have a planner, and that the evidence of purposefulness required an intelligent creator. His contention was that there is an abundance of evidence for the existence of a watchmaker.

Spiral galaxy

Cross-section of *nautilus* shell.

Bishop Paley pointed out the existence of the many living creatures that are vastly more complex and wondrously designed than a watch. He maintained that their origin could only be accounted for by the existence of an intelligent creator who designed and created them. His arguments were never

95

refuted, but with the publication, in 1859, of Darwin's book on evolution, and the steady infiltration of evolutionary thinking, Bishop Paley's arguments were simply forgotten or ignored. Today, we are just beginning to understand how infinitely complex living creatures really are—even the tiniest microscopic forms of life. Bishop Paley's arguments are much stronger today than they were 200 years ago, for we can point out many examples of creatures whose origins could not possibly be accounted for by the random, chance, accidental processes of evolution.

The Bombardier Beetle

The bombardier beetle is found throughout the temperate zone of the world. He is approximately one-half inch long, and has a marvelously complex and highly effective defense mechanism. When an enemy or a predator gets in just the right position, this little beetle shoots very hot, irritating gases out of twin combustion tubes in his tail.

A series of photographs published in the Time-Life publication, *The Insects* (Time-Life Books, New York, 1962), shows a toad approaching a bombardier beetle with the idea of having him for lunch. The bombardier beetle has far different ideas, however. Just as the toad opens his mouth to snatch the bombardier beetle, the beetle swivels his combustion tubes around, and at precisely the right moment, BOOM! The expression on the face of the toad is incredible! His tongue is hanging out, he's gagging, and he's back-pedalling as fast as he can go! The little bombardier beetle, on the other hand, is walking away calm as can be.

When scientists first discovered the bombardier beetle (scientific name is *Brachinus*), they were curious to find out how he accomplished this amazing feat. A number of scientists, including Dr. Hermann Schildknecht, worked on an understanding of the processes involved. It was necessary to perform microsurgery on the beetles, in order to investigate the type of apparatus employed, and chemicals were extracted

96

from the apparatus to discover what kind of chemistry the bombardier beetles used.

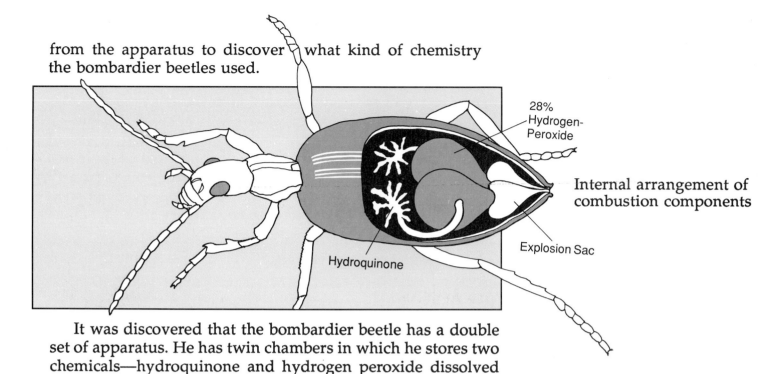

28%
Hydrogen-
Peroxide

Internal arrangement of combustion components

Explosion Sac

Hydroquinone

It was discovered that the bombardier beetle has a double set of apparatus. He has twin chambers in which he stores two chemicals—hydroquinone and hydrogen peroxide dissolved in water. If a chemist mixes these two chemicals, the hydrogen peroxide oxidizes the hydroquinone and the mixture looks like brown soup. The bombardier beetle adds a mysterious inhibitor which prevents the hydrogen peroxide from oxidizing the hydroquinone. In the beetle, this mixture of chemicals is combined with no reaction at all. The solution remains crystal clear.

When the bombardier beetle is threatened and needs to employ his miniature cannon, he squirts the solution of chemicals from the two storage chambers into the two combustion tubes. In the combustion tubes, the beetle provides two enzymes—catalase and peroxidase (a catalyst which makes a chemical reaction happen very rapidly, without any change in the catalyst). Thus, a catalyst may be used over and over again—sometimes a billion times or more a minute. In all living creatures, from bacteria to humans, these catalysts are composed of proteins, and are called enzymes.

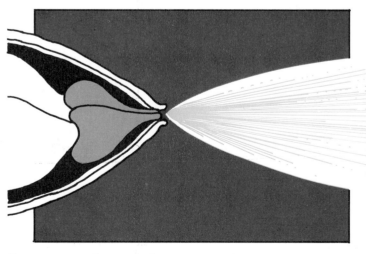

The explosive gases are shot out at a temperature of 212° F.

Catalase is an enzyme that causes the extremely rapid conversion of hydrogen peroxide into water and oxygen. The peroxidase enzyme then causes the oxygen to very rapidly oxidize the hydroquinone into another chemical, called quinone, which is a noxious, or irritating chemical. All of this happens extremely fast in the bombardier beetle's combustion tubes, heating the liquid and gases up to 212 degrees Fahrenheit, and generating a lot of pressure. When the pressure gets high enough, the bombardier beetle opens the valves on the end of his combustion tubes, and the hot gases shoot out with great force. A "pop" can actually be heard as the gases shoot out! The bombardier beetle can repeat the explosion 15 or 20 times in just a few minutes. He can swivel his combustion tubes around 360 degrees, and he never misses!

You can see that the bombardier beetle has a very complicated apparatus. He must have storage chambers, where he stores two very special chemicals. Furthermore, he must supply an inhibitor, especially designed to prevent the two chemicals from reacting with one another. This inhibitor is believed to be a protein, so it is a very large and complicated molecule. The combustion tubes are also special. They must be composed of materials that have the ability to be unaffected by corrosive chemicals heated to 212 degrees Fahrenheit, and they must also be constructed so that they will not rupture under high pressure, and they must be equipped with valves which can be exactly controlled, so the pressure can be released at just the right moment. The bombardier beetle must also have a marvelously designed set of muscles, that enable him to very swiftly and accurately swivel the combustion tubes in the right direction. And, most important of all, the combustion tubes must be supplied with two enzymes—catalase and peroxidase, without which the whole process will fail. Everything has to be in exact working order, at precisely the right time.

How did the little bombardier beetle get such a marvelously complex and perfectly functioning apparatus? Evolutionists must necessarily believe that a bombardier beetle evolved from an ordinary beetle by a series of thousands of genetic mistakes (mutations). On the other hand, the creationist points out that nothing as complicated as the above delineated processes could ever come about by a series of accidents, *especially since nothing works until everything works.*

Let me illustrate: Let us suppose that millions of years ago there was this little beetle (we'll call him Beetle Bailey, or B.B.). One day his mom and dad gave him a chemistry set for his birthday. This chemistry set included all kinds of chemicals,

"Nothing Works Until Everything Works."

Until all parts are operational, in the correct order and fuel is added, the train cannot function.

including hydrogen peroxide and hydroquinone, and even a few enzymes, including catalase and peroxidase. Sometime after getting his chemistry set, B.B. was down in his basement chemistry lab experimenting with chemicals. Suddenly he wondered what would happen if he mixed hydrogen peroxide, hydroquinone, catalase, and peroxidase. So he combined them all in a test tube, and BOOM! That's right—the mess blew up and splattered poor little B.B. all over the walls and ceiling of his chemistry lab. Here's the first problem for evolution: B.B. needs to warn his offspring that little beetles shouldn't do such things, but he can't do that, because he didn't live to produce any offspring! And, therefore, millions of generations and many millions of years, little beetles were blowing themselves up—BOOM, BOOM, BOOM!

Some little beetle had to guess that he should store the two chemicals completely away from the two enzymes. To do this, of course, he must have storage chambers. But why would he invent storage chambers before he had the two chemicals? But on the other hand, what would he do with the two chemicals until he had some place to store them? And, of course, the two chemicals and the storage chambers would be of no use at all until the inhibitor was developed to prevent the chemicals from reacting with each other and making brown soup. On the other hand, how would he know to invent the inhibitor until he had the two chemicals that needed to be inhibited? However, if we suppose that B.B. did manage, by some mysterious process, to invent the two chemicals, the inhibitor, and the storage chambers, what is he going to do with this mixture of chemicals? The enzymes have not been developed yet, so the chemicals won't explode and generate heat and irritating gases. The chemicals will just sit and corrode his innards without the enyzmes, but why would he develop the enzymes before he had the chemicals? On the other hand, why would he develop

If even one element of the sequence is out of order...BOOM!

99

the chemicals, the inhibitor, and the storage chamber until he had the enzymes?

What if B.B. did develop the two enzymes? Has Beetle Bailey become Bombardier Beetle? He has the two chemicals, the inhibitor, the storage chambers, and the two enzymes, which can easily neutralize the inhibitor and cause the two chemicals to explode. B.B. mixes all of this up, and—BOOM! He blows himself up! He hasn't yet invented the combustion tubes! All he has are storage chambers, but no outlet valves, etc. Again, BOOM! BOOM! BOOM! For millions of years, little beetles keep blowing themselves up.

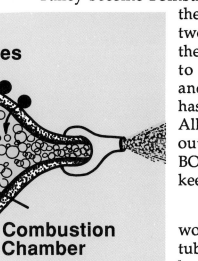

Enzymes

Hydro-guinones + Hydrogen Peroxide

Combustion Chamber

Cross section of combustion tubes.

Many thousands of genes in the beetle would be required to specify a combustion tube designed to do what it must do in the bombardier beetle. It would take engineers many years to produce such a tube, especially if they had to work with materials produced by a beetle. It is impossible that one of the beetle's combustion tubes could be produced by genetic mistakes.

In spite of all of these impossibilities, let us suppose that by some miracle a beetle did manage to invent the two chemicals, the inhibitor, the storage chambers, the enzymes, and the combustion tubes. Is Beetle Bailey finally Bombardier Beetle? What about his communications network? He has no way of giving the right signal at the right time. How will he know the difference between friend and foe? A few miscommunications to the combustion tubes and B.B. is going to lose a lot of friends.

In order to be Bombardier Beetle, B.B. needs everything complete right at the start, but why would he invent the communication network that carries the messages, that, just at the right time, causes the combustion tubes to swivel around so they are pointed at the target, squirting the chemicals into the combustion tubes, and releasing the valves on the combustion tubes? Of what possible use would all that complicated message system be until all the apparatus is complete? On the other hand, what possible use would all those chemicals and special apparatus be until B.B. had the communication network? *Everything* had to be complete and functioning before *anything* would be of any use.

100

Evolutionists believe that the bombardier beetle evolved from an ordinary beetle, and that the change was slow and gradual, and employed many genetic mistakes (or mutations). Most mutations are bad. In fact, there is no scientific evidence that supports the evolutionary idea of so-called "good" mutations. Since all mutations are bad, evolution is impossible!

Furthermore, evolutionists must believe that somehow each intermediate beetle not only managed to survive, but was superior to the preceding form. Thus, according to evolution theory, a long series of genetic mistakes, or mutations, gradually changed the ordinary beetle into a bombardier beetle. Even though none of the intermediates was a bombardier beetle, each intermediate not only survived, but was somehow superior to the preceding stage. To believe that the incredibly complex functions necessary in the bombardier beetle came about as a result of genetic accidents, is, at best, pure fabrication.

Woodpecker skull

The Woodpecker

Some people may think that a woodpecker is hardly more than an ordinary bird. However, the woodpecker is very specially constructed, and, in reality, resembles a miniature jackhammer. It takes a lot of force to drill into concrete, and the jackhammer and the man operating it, especially the jackhammer, take a beating. How does the woodpecker ram his bill into a tree thousands of times a minute without breaking his beak and smashing his brains? And, after all the work of drilling a hole in a tree, how does he manage to reach inside the tree and pull out the bugs for his lunch? But more important still, how do evolutionists explain how an ordinary bird could evolve into a woodpecker?

First of all, a woodpecker must have a special kind of bill. It must be strong and sharp enough to dig into a tree without folding up like an accordion. A woodpecker also has to have a firm grip on the tree into which he is drilling. He does not perch on a limb. He has very stiff tail feathers, which he uses to brace himself against the tree, and specially designed feet, with four claw-like toes. Two toes point forward, or up, and two toes point backward, or down—an arrangement which allows him to get a good, tight grip.

What keeps the woodpecker's brain from rattling around in his skull while his head takes the awful battering necessary to drill a hole? His head is equipped with shock absorbers! These shock absorbers cushion the blows, so that the skull and brain of the woodpecker suffer no damage.

The most amazing thing about the woodpecker is his tongue. It must be very long, because the woodpecker must be able to reach deep into the tree with his tongue, in order to reach bugs and worms. To be able to snatch these insects, the tongue of the woodpecker is equipped with special glands that secrete a sticky substance. Thus, the bugs stick to his tongue just like flies to flypaper. The woodpecker pulls the insects from the tree, which are stuck in the "glue," then pulls in his long tongue and scrapes the bugs off into his mouth.

What does the woodpecker do with such a long tongue? He can't just roll it up and store it in his beak—he might choke to death on it. The Creator has provided a very unique solution to a very unique problem. The tongue of an ordinary bird is anchored in the back of the beak, but this won't work for the woodpecker, because his tongue is too long. Therefore, the tongue of the woodpecker is anchored in the right nostril! The tongue is actually in two halves. After it emerges from the right nostril, it splits into two halves. Each half passes over each side of the skull underneath the skin, comes around and up underneath the beak, and enters the beak through a hole in the beak. Here the two halves combine. Thus, when the woodpecker is not using his long tongue, he rolls it up and stores it in the right nostril.

How could this special arrangement for the woodpecker's tongue have evolved, if, in the beginning, as ordinary birds, his tongue was anchored in the back of the beak? How did it manage to move into the right nostril? If the anchor suddenly hopped from the back of the beak up into the right nostril, the tongue would be too short. On the other hand, would it slowly migrate from the back of the beak up into the right nostril? And, during all of the intermediate stages, would the tongue have been long enough to reach the bugs inside a tree so the woodpecker could eat and survive?

Supposing a bird developed a long tongue anchored in the right nostril, but he did not develop a strong, sharp beak, or the powerful neck muscles, the shock absorbers, and the special toes and claws. What possible use could such a bird make of the long tongue without the other apparatus employed by the woodpecker? On the other hand, suppose a bird developed all that special apparatus needed to drill a hole in a tree, but not the long tongue. He would spend all day drilling a hole in a tree in anticipation of a meal of insects, but after all the hard work, he would not be able to reach the bugs or worms. Again, you see, nothing works until everything works. The woodpecker did not, and could not have evolved. Only God could create a woodpecker.

Archer Fish

The archer fish performs a rather remarkable feat. He positions himself under a branch overhanging the water on which he sees an insect. He slowly and carefully rises until he is just under the surface of the water, and then shoots water out of his mouth and knocks the bug into the water. Before the insect can get away, the archer fish eats him. The eyes of the archer fish are under the water when he does this, and since refraction of light is different in water than

it is in air, the bug appears to be in a slightly different position than he actually is. However, the archer fish knows how to adjust for this difference, as he is always on target. As in the case of the woodpecker, it would be very difficult to explain how this behavior and ability could have evolved by a series of genetic accidents!

103

Trilobite Eyes

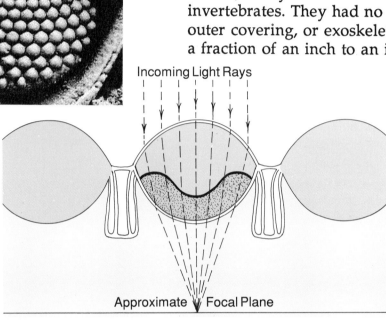

Close up of fossil trilobite eye showing compound structure.

Incoming Light Rays

Approximate Focal Plane

Trilobite eye showing double lens construction.

The trilobite is a creature that has long been extinct, but gives marvelous testimony to the creative power of God, and demonstrates the foolishness of belief in evolution. Trilobites had three sections, or lobes—thus the name tri-lobe-ite. Evolutionists believe they became extinct about 200 million years ago, but most creation scientists believe they probably became extinct as a result of, or soon after, Noah's Flood, only *thousands* of years ago. Trilobites were invertebrates. They had no internal skeleton, but had a tough outer covering, or exoskeleton. Many were very small—from a fraction of an inch to an inch long—but some were as long as 12 inches. They lived on the bottom of shallow seas, and most had eyes.

The eyes of the trilobite were the most remarkable feature about these animals. Scientists have been able to study the optics of the trilobite eyes. The lenses of our eyes are composed of living, organic tissues, so they rapidly decompose after death. The lenses of trilobite eyes, however, were composed of inorganic, crystalline calcium carbonate, or calcite. Thus, the lenses of the trilobite eyes were still intact in the fossil remains recovered by paleontologists. Most of the fascinating research on trilobite eyes was performed by Dr. Riccardo Levi-Setti, a professor at the University of Chicago.

The first significant thing about these eyes is that they have a double lens. Each one of our eyes has only a single lens. In order to see under water without distortion, however, you must have a double lens in each eye, and that is precisely what the trilobite had. The most incredible thing about the trilobite eye, however, is the fact that it produced perfect, undistorted vision. Dr. Levi-Setti discovered that the trilobites had "solved" Abbe's Sine Law, Fermat's Principle, and other laws and principles of optics, and had perfectly constructed crystalline lenses so that there was no distortion at all. The scientists studying these eyes proclaimed that these eyes looked as if they had been designed by a physicist!

104

They went on to say what a wonderful thing evolution can do, instead of giving God, the greatest physicist of all, the credit for creating those perfect eyes. Evolutionists deny the obvious, because, if they admit such exquisite design demands a Designer, then they are brought face to face with the Creator God.

No Excuse for Unbelief

The Bible tells us that no one has an excuse for not believing that God is the Master and Creator of all things:

For the invisible things of Him from the creation of the world are clearly seen, being understood by the things that are made, even His eternal power and Godhead; so that they are without excuse.

Romans 1:20

No one has an excuse, because from the things that God has created, we can easily see evidence of His existence, of His divine power, of His infinite intelligence, and of His divinity. God gave the scientists who studied the trilobites undeniable evidence of the existence of an

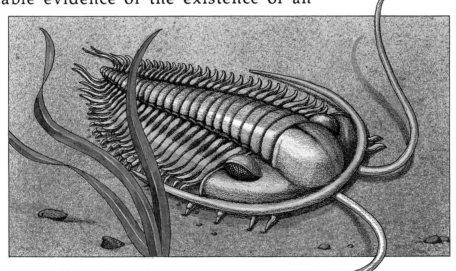

One of many species of trilobites.

incredibly intelligent Designer, certainly vastly more intelligent than any human. It was only after many years of study that scientists discovered the laws and principles of optics, but they did not invent those laws and principles. God, the Creator of the universe, created all the natural laws and processes that man has discovered.

Glory to God, the Creator!

All of God's creation gives an abundance of evidence that He has created it, for which we praise Him.

Know ye that the LORD He is God: It is He that hath made us, and not we ourselves; we are His people, and the sheep of His pasture.

Psalm 100:3

We have seen that the universe could not have created itself; that it is impossible for stars to form spontaneously by themselves. God created them, by His mighty power!

The heavens declare the glory of God; and the firmament (space) showeth His handiwork.

Psalm 19:1

From our studies concerning the fossil record, embryology, comparative anatomy, and the indescribable complexity and organization of living creatures, we see that each one testifies to the creative genius of God that passes all understanding.

But ask now the beasts, and they shall teach thee; and the fowls of the air, and they shall tell thee:

Or speak to the earth, and it shall teach thee: And the fishes of the sea shall declare unto thee.

Who knoweth not in all these that the hand of the Lord hath wrought this?

Job 12:7-9

We praise God for the wonderful universe He has created and for the beautiful earth He prepared for our home. We thank Him for the precious life He has given to each of us, and, most of all, we thank and praise Him for our Savior, the Lord Jesus Christ.

Thou art worthy, O Lord, to receive glory and honor and power: For Thou hast created all things, and for Thy pleasure they are and were created.

Revelation 4:11

Glossary

Algae — one-celled organisms or many-celled organisms, which contain chlorophyll, found in the form of colonies, filaments, or sheets.

Ammonia — a caustic gas, NH_3.

Amphibian — an animal, such as a toad, frog, or salamander, that spends time both in water and on land and that lays its eggs in water or wet soil.

Astronomer — a scientist who studies stars, galaxies, asteroids, comets, planets, moons, and other objects in the sky.

Bacteria — one-celled, microscopic organisms with no organized nucleus.

Big Bang Theory — the evolutionary theory of the origin of the universe that says that billions of years ago all the energy and matter in the universe was in the form of a superdense, superhot plasma ball (the "cosmic egg") of sub-atomic particles and radiation which exploded in a "big bang" that gave rise to hydrogen and helium gases which then evolved into the universe as we know it today.

Brachiopods — sea animals with symmetrical bivalve shells.

Chromosome — threadlike body in the nucleus, rich in DNA and bearing the genetic information of the cell.

DNA — deoxyribonucleic acid which is constructed by combining nucleotides in long chains. Most genes consist of many thousands of nucleotides.

Galaxy — a huge group of stars (it is estimated that each galaxy contains about 100 billion stars).

Helium — a gas of atomic weight 4, the second lightest element in the universe, next to hydrogen.

Hydrogen — a gas of atomic weight 1 — the lightest element in the universe.

Immutable — unchangeable.

Invertebrate — an animal that either has a soft body (such as a worm or a jellyfish) or which has either a hard outer shell (such as an oyster,) which has a firm outer covering called an exoskeleton with a soft inner body (such as a beetle).

Nucleotide — a building block for nucleic acids such as DNA and RNA. It is made of the union of a sugar, phosphate and an organic base such as adenine, cytosine, guanine, thymine, or guanine.

Photosynthesis — the complex process whereby green plants and certain algae and bacteria absorb visible light and convert the light into chemical energy for growth and reproduction.

Protein — a large and complex molecule formed by combining amino acids in a long chain (average length 400 amino acids). Proteins make up some of the most vitally important substances in our body. For example: Hemoglobin is the protein in red blood cells that binds oxygen; human growth hormone is a protein; antibodies are proteins; enzymes, those marvelous catalysts in plants and animals that make chemical reactions accelerate and without which life would be impossible, are proteins. Many other vitally important substances in living things are proteins.

Protozoa — one-celled, usually microscopic organisms with organized nucleus and with various modes of locomotion.

Quasar — a name derived from the term "quasi-stellar object." Astronomers do not really know what these objects are. They are known to be very hot, energetic stellar (star-like) objects.

RNA — ribonucleic acid. The nucleotides which are combined in the long chains which make up RNA are composed of a sugar (ribose), phosphoric acid, and either a pyrimidine or a purine. There are several different types of these important molecules, each having a vitally important function.

Sea urchins — an invertebrate sea animal having a flattened globular body of fused plates covered with a spiny skin.

Solar System — the sun and all objects that orbit the sun, such as the planets, comets, and asteroids, and the moons that orbit the planets.

Supernova — the explosive destruction of a star.

Ultraviolet light — light of very short wave given off by the sun that has very high energy and is invisible to the human eye.

Transitional form — in evolutionary theory, a plant or animal changes or evolves gradually into a different kind of plant or animal, passing through many intermediate or partway stages. For example, evolutionists believe the fins of fishes gradually changed into the feet and legs of amphibians. Something partway between a fish and an amphibian possessing part fins and part feet would be a transitional form.

Trilobite — an invertebrate sea animal, now believed to be extinct, that had a body composed of three lobes and enclosed in a hard exoskeleton, or case.

Vertebrate — an animal with an internal skeleton and backbone such as fishes, amphibians, reptiles, birds, and mammals.

Index

CREDITS

Gloria Clanin . . . . Production Director

Ron Hight . . . . Art Director

Connie Horn . . . . Editor

Ruth Richards . . . . Typesetting